Prehistoric Men

BY

ROBERT J. BRAIDWOOD

RESEARCH ASSOCIATE, OLD WORLD PREHISTORY

PROFESSOR
ORIENTAL INSTITUTE AND DEPARTMENT OF ANTHROPOLOGY
UNIVERSITY OF CHICAGO

Drawings by SUSAN T. RICHERT

CHICAGO NATURAL HISTORY MUSEUM

POPULAR SERIES

ANTHROPOLOGY, NUMBER 37

Preface

Like the writing of most professional archeologists, mine has been confined to so-called learned papers. Good, bad, or indifferent, these papers were in a jargon that only my colleagues and a few advanced students could understand. Hence, when I was asked to do this little book, I soon found it extremely difficult to say what I meant in simple fashion. The style is new to me, but I hope the reader will not find it forced or pedantic; at least I have done my very best to tell the story simply and clearly.

Many friends have aided in the preparation of the book. The whimsical charm of Miss Susan Richert's illustrations add enormously to the spirit I wanted. She gave freely of her own time on the drawings and in planning the book with me. My colleagues at the University of Chicago, especially Professor Wilton M. Krogman (now of the University of Pennsylvania), and also Mrs. Linda Braidwood, Associate of the Oriental Institute, and Professors Fay-Cooper Cole and Sol Tax, of the Department of Anthropology, gave me counsel in matters bearing on their special fields, and the Department of Anthropology bore some of the expense of the illustrations. From Mrs. Irma Hunter and Mr. Arnold Maremont, who are not archeologists at all and have only an intelligent layman's notion of archeology, I had sound advice on how best to tell the story. I am deeply indebted to all these friends.

While I was preparing the second edition, I had the great fortune to be able to rework the third chapter with Professor Sherwood L. Washburn, now of the Department of Anthropology of the University of California, and the fourth, fifth, and

· 3 ·

sixth chapters with Professor Hallum L. Movius, Jr., of the Peabody Museum, Harvard University. The book has gained greatly in accuracy thereby. In matters of dating, Professor Movius and the indications of Professor W. F. Libby's Carbon 14 chronology project have both encouraged me to choose the lowest dates now current for the events of the Pleistocene Ice Age. There is still no certain way of fixing a direct chronology for most of the Pleistocene, but Professor Libby's method appears very promising for its end range and for proto-historic dates. In any case, this book names "periods," and new dates may be written in against mine, if new and better dating systems appear.

I wish to thank Dr. Clifford C. Gregg, Director of Chicago Natural History Museum, for the opportunity to publish this book. My old friend, Dr. Paul S. Martin, Chief Curator in the Department of Anthropology, asked me to undertake the job and inspired me to complete it. I am also indebted to Miss Lillian A. Ross, Associate Editor of Scientific Publications, and to Mr. George I. Quimby, Curator of Exhibits in Anthropology, for all the time they have given me in getting the manuscript into proper shape.

ROBERT J. BRAIDWOOD

June 15, 1950

Preface to the Sixth Edition

In preparing the enlarged later editions, many of the above mentioned friends have again helped me. I have picked the brains of Professor F. Clark Howell of the Department of Anthropology of the University of Chicago in reworking the earlier chapters, and the advice of such European colleagues as Professors François Bordes, Carl-Axel Moberg, and Luis Pericot Garcia has been invaluable to me.

All of Mrs. Susan Richert Allen's original drawings appear, but a few necessary corrections have been made in some of the charts and some new drawings have been added by Mr. John Pfiffner, formerly Staff Artist. Chicago Natural History Museum.

ROBERT J. BRAIDWOOD

July 1, 1963

Contents

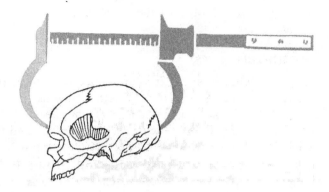

HOW WE LEARN about Prehistoric Men

Prehistory means the time before written history began. Actually, more than 99 per cent of man's story is prehistory. Man is probably well over a million years old, but he did not begin to write history (or to write anything) until about 5,000 years ago.

The men who lived in prehistoric times left us no history books, but they did unintentionally leave a record of their presence and their way of life. This record is studied and interpreted by different kinds of scientists.

SCIENTISTS WHO FIND OUT ABOUT PREHISTORIC MEN

The scientists who study the bones and teeth and any other parts they find of the bodies of prehistoric men, are called *physical anthropologists*. Physical anthropologists are trained, much like doctors, to know all about the human body. They study living people, too; they know more about the biological facts of human "races" than anybody else. If the police find a badly decayed body in a trunk, they ask a physical anthropologist to tell them what the person originally looked like.

The physical anthropologists who specialize in prehistoric men work with fossils, so they are sometimes called *human paleontologists.*

ARCHEOLOGISTS

There is a kind of scientist who studies the things that prehistoric men made and did. Such a scientist is called an *archeologist.* It is the archeologist's business to look for the stone and metal tools, the pottery, the graves, and the caves or huts of the men who lived before history began.

But there is more to archeology than just looking for things. In Professor V. Gordon Childe's words, archeology "furnishes a sort of history of human activity, provided always that the actions have produced concrete results and left recognizable material traces." You will see that there are at least three points in what Childe says:

1. The archeologists have to find the traces of things left behind by ancient man, and

2. Only a few objects may be found, for most of these were probably too soft or too breakable to last through the years. However,

3. The archeologist must use whatever he can find to tell a story—to make a "sort of history"—from the objects and living-places and graves that have escaped destruction.

What I mean is this: Let us say you are walking through a dump yard, and you find a rusty old spark plug. If you want to think about what the spark plug means, you quickly remember that it is a part of an automobile motor. This tells you something about the man who threw the spark plug on the dump. He either had an automobile, or he knew or lived near someone who did. He can't have lived so very long ago, you'll remember, because spark plugs and automobiles are only about sixty years old.

When you think about the old spark plug in this way you have just been making the beginnings of what we call an archeological *interpretation;* you have been making the spark plug tell a story. It is the same way with the man-made things we archeologists find and put in museums. Usually, only a few of these objects are pretty to look at; but each of them has some sort of story to tell. Making the interpretation of his finds is the most important part of the archeologist's job. It is the way he gets at the "sort of history of human activity" which is expected of archeology.

SOME OTHER SCIENTISTS

There are many other scientists who help the archeologist and the physical anthropologist find out about prehistoric men. The geologists help us tell the age of the rocks or caves or gravel beds in which human bones or man-made objects are found. There are other scientists with names which all begin with "paleo" (the Greek word for "old"). The *paleontologists* study fossil animals. There are also, for example, such scientists as *paleobotanists* and *paleoclimatologists*, who study ancient plants and climates. These scientists help us to know the kinds of animals and plants that were living in prehistoric times and so could be used for food by ancient man; what the weather was like; and whether there were glaciers. Also, when I tell you that prehistoric men did not appear until long after the great dinosaurs had disappeared, I go on the say-so of the paleontologists. They know that fossils of men and of dinosaurs are not found in the same geological period. The dinosaur fossils come in early periods, the fossils of men much later.

Since World War II even the atomic scientists have been helping the archeologists. By testing the amount of radio-activity left in charcoal, wood, or other vegetable matter obtained from archeological sites, they have been able to date the sites. Shell has been used also, and even the hair of Egyptian mummies. The dates of geological and climatic events have also been discovered. Some of this work has been done from drillings taken from the bottom of the sea.

It has also proved possible to assess the time when certain volcanic rocks were formed. If a bed of such rocks was formed later than (and hence sealed in) an archeological or human

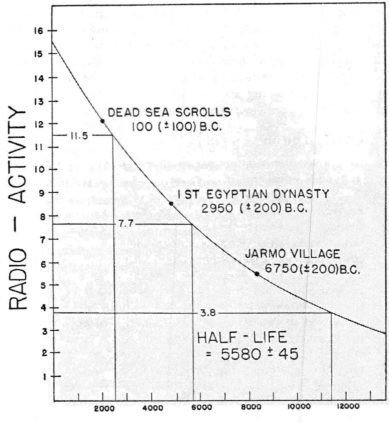

RADIOCARBON CHART

The rate of disappearance of radioactivity as time passes.[1]

[1] It is important that the limitations of the radioactive carbon "dating" system be held in mind. As the statistics involved in the system are used, there are two chances in three that the "date" of the sample falls within the range given as plus or minus an added number of years. For example, the "date" for ·the Jarmo village (see chart), given as 6750 ± 200 B.C., really means that there are only two chances in three that the real date of the charcoal sampled fell between 6950 and 6550 B.C. We have also begun to suspect that there are ways in which the samples themselves may have become "contaminated," either on the early or on the late side. We now tend to be suspicious of single radioactive carbon determinations, or of determinations from one site alone. But as a fabric of consistent determinations for several or more sites of one archeological period becomes available, we gain confidence in them as "dates."

fossil site, then we may say that the site must be at least earlier than the "date" of the covering rock bed. Unfortunately, we do not always find such volcanic beds where we'd like to find them—nicely sealing in our own sites. The method depends on measuring the amount of argon in the rock, the result of potassium-argon transformation. Measurements of less than about 100,000 years ago are difficult to make; so the method deals mainly with traces of early men.

Such dating by radioactivity has considerably changed the dates which the archeologists used to give. If you find that some of the dates I give here are more recent (or more ancient) than the dates you see in other books on prehistory, it is because I am using one of the new dating systems.

HOW THE SCIENTISTS FIND OUT

So far, this chapter has been mainly about the people who find out about prehistoric men. We also need a word about *how* they find out.

All our finds came by accident until about a hundred years ago. Men digging wells, or digging in caves for fertilizer, often turned up ancient swords or pots or stone arrowheads. People also found some odd pieces of stone that didn't look like natural forms, but they also didn't look like any known tool. As a result, the people who found them gave them queer names; for example, "thunderbolts." The people thought the strange stones came to earth as bolts of lightning. We know now that these strange stones were prehistoric stone tools.

Many important finds still come to us by accident. In 1935, a British dentist, A. T. Marston, found the first of two fragments of a very important fossil human skull, in a gravel pit at Swanscombe, on the River Thames, England. He had to wait nine months, until the face of the gravel pit had been dug eight yards farther back, before the second fragment appeared. They fitted! Then, twenty years later, still another piece appeared. In 1928 workmen who were blasting out rock for the breakwater in the port of Haifa began to notice flint tools. Thus the story of cave men on Mount Carmel, in Palestine, began to be known.

Planned archeological digging is only about a century old. Even before this, however, a few men realized the significance of objects they dug from the ground; one of these early archeologists was our own Thomas Jefferson. An early digger of mounds was a German grocer's clerk, Heinrich Schliemann. Schliemann made a fortune as a merchant, first in Europe and then in the California gold-rush of 1849. He became an American citizen. Then he retired and had both money and time to test an old idea of his. He believed that the heroes of ancient Troy and Mycenae were once real Trojans and Greeks. He proved it by going to Turkey and Greece and digging up the mounds that contained the remains of both cities.

Schliemann had the great good fortune to find rich and spectacular treasures, and he also had the common sense to keep notes and make descriptions of what he found. He proved beyond doubt that many ancient city mounds can be *stratified*. This means that there may be the remains of many towns in a mound, one above another, like layers in a cake.

You might like to have an idea of how mounds come to be in layers. The original settlers may have chosen the spot because it had a good spring and there were good fertile lands nearby, or perhaps because it was close to some road or river or harbor. These settlers probably built their town of stone and mud-brick. Finally, something would have happened to the town—a flood, or a burning, or a raid by enemies—and the walls of the houses would have fallen in or would have melted down as mud in the rain. Nothing would have remained but the mud and debris of a low mound of *one* layer.

The second settlers would have wanted the spot for the same reasons the first settlers did—good water, land, and roads. Also, the second settlers would have found a nice low mound to build their houses on, a protection from floods. But again, something would finally have happened to the second town, and the walls of *its* houses would have come tumbling down. This makes the *second* layer. And so on. . . .

In Syria I once had the good fortune to dig on a large mound that had no less than fifteen layers. Also, most of the layers were thick, and there were signs of rebuilding and repairs within each layer. The mound was more than a hundred feet high. In each layer, the building material used had been a soft, unbaked mud-brick, and most of the debris consisted of fallen or rain-melted mud from these mud-bricks.

This idea of *stratification*, like the cake layers, was already a familiar one to the geologists by Schliemann's time. They could show that their lowest layer of rock was oldest or earliest, and that the overlying layers became more recent as one moved upward. Schliemann's digging proved the same thing at Troy. His first (lowest and earliest) city had at least nine layers above it; he thought that the second layer contained the remains of Homer's Troy. We now know that Homeric Troy was layer VIIa from the bottom; also, we count eleven layers or sub-layers in total.

Schliemann's work marks the beginnings of modern archeology in southwestern Asia. Scholars soon set out to dig on ancient sites, from Egypt to Central America.

ARCHEOLOGICAL INFORMATION

As time went on, the study of archeological materials—found either by accident or by digging on purpose—began to show certain things. Archeologists began to get ideas as to the kinds of objects that belonged together. If you compared a mail-order catalogue of 1890 with one of today, you would see a lot of differences. If you really studied the two catalogues hard, you would also begin to see that certain objects "go together." Horseshoes and metal buggy tires and pieces of harness would begin to fit into a picture with certain kinds of coal stoves and furniture and china dishes and kerosene lamps. Our friend the spark plug, and radios and electric refrigerators and light bulbs would fit into a picture with different kinds of furniture and dishes and tools. You won't be old enough to remember the kind of hats that women wore in 1890, but you've probably seen pictures of them, and you know very well they couldn't be worn today.

This is one of the ways that archeologists study their materials. The various tools and weapons and jewelry, the pottery, the kinds of houses, and even the ways of burying the dead tend to fit into pictures. Some archeologists call all of the things that go together to make such a picture an *assemblage*. The assemblage of the first layer of Schliemann's Troy was even more different from that of the seventh layer than our 1900 mail-order catalogue is from the one of today.

The archeologists who came after Schliemann began to notice other things and to compare them with occurrences in modern times. The idea that people will buy better mouse-traps goes back into very ancient times. Today, if we make good automobiles or radios, we can sell some of them in Turkey or even in Timbuktu. This means that a few present-day types of American automobiles and radios form part of present-day "assemblages" in both Turkey and Timbuktu. The total present-day "assemblage" of Turkey is quite different from that of Timbuktu or that of America, but they have at least some automobiles and some radios in common.

Now these automobiles and radios will eventually wear out. Let us suppose we could go to some remote part of Turkey or to Timbuktu in a dream. We don't know what the date is, in our dream, but we see all sorts of strange things and ways of living in both places. Nobody tells us what the date is. But suddenly we see a 1940 Ford; so we know that in our dream it has to be at least the year 1940, and only as many years after that as we could reasonably expect a Ford to keep in running order. The Ford would probably break down in twenty years' time, so the Turkish or Timbuktu "assemblage" we're seeing in our dream has to date at about A.D. 1940–60.

Archeologists not only "date" their ancient materials in this way; they also see over what distances and between which peoples trading was done. It turns out that there was a good deal of trading in ancient times, probably all on a barter and exchange basis.

EVERYTHING BEGINS TO FIT TOGETHER

Now we need to pull all these ideas together and see the complicated structure the archeologists can build with their materials.

Even the earliest archeologists soon found that there was a very long range of prehistoric time which would yield only very simple things. For this very long early part of prehistory, there was little to be found but the flint tools which wandering, hunting and gathering people made, and the bones of the wild animals they ate. Toward the end of prehistoric time there was a general settling down with the coming of agriculture, and all sorts of new things began to be made. Archeologists soon got a general notion of what ought to appear with what. Thus, it would upset a French prehistorian digging at the bottom of a very early cave if he found a fine bronze sword, just as much as it would upset him if he found a beer bottle. The people of his very early cave layer simply could not have made bronze swords, which came later, just as do beer bottles. Some accidental disturbance of the layers of his cave must have happened.

With any luck, archeologists do their digging in a layered, stratified site. They find the remains of everything that would last through time, in several different layers. They know that the assemblage in the bottom layer was laid down earlier than the assemblage in the next layer above, and so on up to the topmost layer, which is the latest. They look at the results of other "digs" and find that some other archeologist 200 miles away has found ax-heads in his lowest layer, exactly like the ax-heads of their fifth layer. This means that their fifth layer must have been lived in at about the same time as was the first layer in the site 200 miles away. It also may mean that the people who lived in the two layers knew and traded with each other. Or it could mean that they didn't necessarily know each other, but simply that both traded with a third group at about the same time.

You can see that the more we dig and find, the more clearly the main facts begin to stand out. We begin to be more sure of which peoples lived at the same time, which earlier and which later. We begin to know who traded with whom, and which peoples seemed to live off by themselves. We begin to find enough skeletons in burials so that the physical anthropologists can tell us what the people looked like. We get animal bones, and a paleontologist may tell us they are all bones of wild animals; or he may tell us that some or most of the bones are those of domesticated animals, for instance, sheep or cattle, and therefore the people must have kept herds.

More important than anything else—as our structure grows more complicated and our materials increase—is the fact that "a sort of history of human activity" does begin to appear. The habits or traditions that men formed in the making of their tools and in the ways they did things, begin to stand out for us. How characteristic were these habits and traditions? What areas did they spread over? How long did they last? We watch the different tools and the traces of the way things were done—how the burials were arranged, what the living-places were like, and so on. We wonder about the people themselves, for the traces of habits and traditions are useful to us only as clues to the men who once had them. So we ask the physical anthropologists about the skeletons that we found in the burials. The physical anthropologists tell us about the anatomy and the similarities and differences which the skeletons show when compared with other skeletons. The physical anthropologists are even working on a method—chemical tests of the bones—that may enable them to discover what the blood-type may have been. One thing is sure. We have never found a group of skeletons so absolutely similar among themselves—so cast from a single mould, so to speak—that we could claim to have a "pure" race. I am sure we never shall.

We become particularly interested in any signs of change—when new materials and tool types and ways of doing things replace old ones. We watch for signs of social change and progress in one way or another.

We must do all this without one word of written history to aid us. Everything we are concerned with goes back to the time *before* men learned to write. That is the prehistorian's job—to find out what happened before history began.

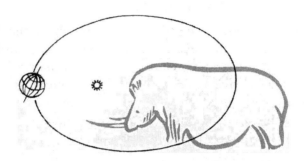

THE CHANGING WORLD in which Prehistoric Men Lived

Mankind, we'll say, is at least a million years old. The potassium-argon age determination we spoke of above may yet make the figure closer to two million years. But, since we also still have to face the problem of when we shall speak of man as *man*, let us take the one million years as a good round figure to work with. It is very hard to understand how long a time a million years really is. If we were to compare this whole length of time to one day, we'd get something like this: The present time is midnight, and Jesus was born just two minutes and fifty seconds ago. Earliest history began about seven minutes ago. Everything before 11:53 P.M. was in prehistoric time.

Or maybe we can grasp the length of time better in terms of generations. As you know, primitive peoples tend to marry and have children rather early in life. So suppose we say that twenty years will make an average generation. At this rate there would be 50,000 generations in a million years. But our United States is much less than ten generations old, twenty-five generations take us back before the time of Columbus, Julius Caesar was alive just 100 generations ago,

David was king of Israel less than 150 generations ago, 250 generations take us back to the beginning of written history. And there were 49,750 generations of men before written history began!

CHANGES IN ENVIRONMENT

The earth probably hasn't changed much in the last 5,000 years (250 generations). Men have built things on its surface and dug into it and drawn boundaries on maps of it, but the places where rivers, lakes, seas, and mountains now stand have changed very little. In fact, such changes as there have been within the last 5,000 years have probably depended as much on the activities of men as upon nature.

In earlier times the earth looked very different. Geologists call the last great geological period the *Pleistocene*. It began about two million years ago, if the potassium-argon age determination method proves trustworthy. It was a time of great fluctuation and change in climates, land forms and environments. Sometimes we call it the Ice Age, for in the Pleistocene there were at least three or four times when large areas of earth were covered with glaciers. The reason for my uncertainty is that while there seem to have been four major mountain or alpine phases of glaciation, there may only have been three general continental phases in the Old World.[1]

Glaciers are great sheets of ice, sometimes over a thousand feet thick, which are now known only in Greenland and Antarctica and in high mountains. During several of the glacial periods in the Ice Age, the glaciers covered most of

[1] This is a complicated affair and I do not want to bother you with its details. Both the alpine and the continental ice sheets seem to have had minor fluctuations during their *main* phases, and the advances of the later phases destroyed many of the traces of the earlier phases. The general textbooks have tended to follow the names and numbers established for the Alps early in this century by two German geologists. I will not bother you with the names, but there were *four* major phases. It is the second of these alpine phases which seems to fit the traces of the earliest of the great continental glaciations. In this book, I will use the four-part system, since it is the most familiar, but will add the word *alpine* so you may remember to make the transition to the continental system if you wish to do so.

· 18 ·

Canada and the northern United States and reached down into England and northern Germany in Europe. Smaller ice sheets sat like caps on the Rockies, the Alps, and the Himalayas. The continental glaciation only happened north of the equator, however, so remember that "Ice Age" is only half true.

As you know, the amount of water on and about the earth does not vary. These large glaciers contained millions of tons of water frozen into ice. Because so much water was frozen and contained in the glaciers, the water level of lakes and oceans was lowered. Flooded areas were drained and appeared as dry land. There were times in the Ice Age when there was no English Channel, so that England was not an island, and a land bridge at the Dardanelles probably divided the Mediterranean from the Black Sea.

A very important thing for people living during the time of a glaciation wa₁ the region adjacent to the glacier. They could not, of course, live on the ice itself. The questions would be how close could they live to it, and how would they have had to change their way of life to do so.

GLACIERS CHANGE THE WEATHER

Great sheets of ice change the weather. When the front of a glacier stood at Milwaukee, the weather must have been bitterly cold in Chicago. The climate of the whole world would have been different, and you can see how animals and men would have been forced to move from one place to another in search of food and warmth.

On the other hand, it looks as if only a minor proportion of the whole Ice Age was really taken up by times of glaciation. In between came the *interglacial* periods. During these times the climate around Chicago was as warm as it is now, and sometimes even warmer. It may interest you to know that the last great glacier melted away less than 10,000 years ago. Professor Ernst Antevs thinks we may be living in an interglacial period and that the Ice Age may not be over yet. So if you want to make a killing in real estate for your several hundred times great-grandchildren, you might buy some land in the Arizona desert or the Sahara.

We do not yet know just why the glaciers appeared and disappeared, as they did. It surely had something to do with an increase in rainfall and a fall in temperature. It probably also had to do with a general tendency for the land to rise at the beginning of the Pleistocene. We know there was some mountain-building at that time. Hence, rain-bearing winds nourished the rising and cooler uplands with snow. An increase in all three of these factors—if they came together— would only have needed to be slight. But exactly why this happened we do not know.

The reason I tell you about the glaciers is simply to remind you of the changing world in which prehistoric men lived. Their surroundings—the animals and plants they used for food, and the weather they had to protect themselves from— were always changing. On the other hand, this change happened over so long a period of time and was so slow that individual people could not have noticed it. Glaciers, about which they probably knew nothing, moved in hundreds of miles to the north of them. The people must simply have wandered ever more southward in search of the plants and animals on which they lived. Or some men may have stayed where they were and learned to hunt different animals and eat different foods. Prehistoric men had to keep adapting themselves to new environments and those who were most adaptive were most successful.

The truly unique thing about men is that gradually, throughout their long prehistory, their adaptations to environments—and to environmental changes—have been accomplished by the tools that men themselves have made and the ways in which men have acted as social groups.

OTHER CHANGES

Changes did, of course, take place in the men themselves as well as in the ways they lived. The major biological changes seem to have taken place during the earlier parts of the Pleistocene, however. As time went on, we find the traces of the better tools and weapons men were making. Then, too, we begin to find signs of how they started thinking of other things than food and the tools to get it with. We find that they painted on the walls of caves, and decorated their tools; we find that they buried their dead.

At about the time when the last great glacier was finally melting away in the more northern regions, men in the Near East made the first basic change in human economy. They began to plant grain, and they learned to raise and herd certain animals. This meant that they could store food in granaries and "on the hoof" against the bad times of the year. This first really basic change in man's way of living has been called the "food-producing revolution." In the New World (in Mesoamerica) the same great discovery was presently made, independently, and on the basis of a quite different set of food plants and without animals. By the time it happened, a modern kind of climate was beginning, but it does *not* appear that change of climate in either the Near East or in Mesoamerica caused the change in ways of living there. Men had already grown to look as they do now. Know-how in ways of living had developed and progressed, slowly but surely, up to a point. It was impossible for men to go beyond that point if they only hunted and fished and gathered wild foods. Once the basic change was made—once the food-producing revolution became effective—technology leaped ahead and civilization and written history soon began.

Prehistoric Men THEMSELVES

DO WE KNOW WHERE MAN ORIGINATED?

For a long time some scientists thought the "cradle of mankind" was in central Asia. Other scientists insisted it was in Africa, and still others said it might have been in Europe. Actually, we don't know where it was. We don't even know that there was only *one* "cradle." If we had to choose a "cradle" at this moment, we would certainly say Africa. But the southern portions of Asia and Europe may also have been included in the general area. The scene of the early development of mankind was certainly the Old World. It is quite certain men didn't reach North or South America until almost the end of the Ice Age—had they done so earlier we would certainly have found some trace of them by now.

The earliest tools we have yet found come from central and south Africa. By the dating system I'm using, these tools must be well over a million years old. There are reports that a few such early tools have been found—at the Sterkfontein and Swartkrans caves in south Africa and at Olduvai in Tanganyika—along with the bones of small fossil men called "australopithecines."

Not all scientists would agree that the australopithecines were "men," or would agree that the tools were made by the australopithecines themselves. For these sticklers, the earliest bones of men come from the island of Java. The date would be somewhat more than a half million years ago. So far, we have not yet found the tools which we suppose these earliest men in the Far East must have made.

Let me say it another way. How old are the earliest traces of men we now have? Over a million years. This was at the time of the first onset of colder conditions in the north, which appear to have marked the beginning of the Pleistocene period. What has been found so far? The tools which the men of those times made, in different parts of Africa. It is now fairly generally agreed that the "men" who made the tools were the australopithecines. More and more finds of several types of australopithecines and their tools are being made at Olduvai. The next earliest bones we have were found in Java, and they may be several hundreds of thousands of years younger than the earliest African finds. We haven't yet found the tools of these early Javanese. Our knowledge of tool-using in Africa spreads quickly as time goes on; soon after the appearance of tools in the south we have them from as far north as Algeria.

Very soon after the earliest Javanese come the bones of slightly more developed people in Java, and the jawbone of a man who once lived in what is now Germany. The same general glacial beds which yielded the later Javanese bones and the German jawbone also include tools. These finds come from the time of the second alpine glaciation.

So this is the situation. By the time of the end of the second alpine or first continental glaciation (say 400,000 years ago) we have traces of men from the extremes of the more southerly portions of the Old World—South Africa, eastern Asia, and western Europe. There are also some traces of men in the middle ground. In fact, Professor Franz Weidenreich believed that creatures who were the immediate ancestors of men had already spread over Europe, Africa, and Asia by the time the Ice Age began. We certainly have no reason to disbelieve this, but fortunate accidents of discovery have not yet given us the evidence to prove it.

MEN AND APES

Many people used to get extremely upset at the ill-formed notion that "man descended from the apes." Such words were much more likely to start fights or "monkey trials" than the correct notion that all living animals, including man, ascended or evolved from a single-celled organism which lived in the primeval seas hundreds of millions of years ago. Men are mammals, of the order called Primates, and man's living relatives are the great apes. Men didn't "descend" from the apes or apes from men, and mankind must have had much closer relatives who have since become extinct.

Men stand erect. They also walk and run on their two feet. Apes are happiest in trees, swinging with their arms from branch to branch. Few branches of trees will hold the mighty gorilla, although he still manages to sleep in trees. Apes can't stand really erect in our sense, and when they have to run on the ground, they use the knuckles of their hands as well as their feet.

The key group of fossil bones here is the south African australopithecines. These are called the *Australopithecinae* or "man-apes" or sometimes even "ape-men." We do not *know* that they were directly ancestral to men but they can hardly have been so to apes. Presently I'll describe them a bit more. The reason I mention them here is that while they had brains no larger than those of apes, their hipbones were enough like ours so that they must have stood erect. There is no good reason to think they couldn't have walked as we do.

BRAINS, HANDS, AND TOOLS

Whether the australopithecines were our ancestors or not, the proper ancestors of men must have been able to stand erect and to walk on their two feet. Three further important things probably were involved, next, before they could become men proper. These are:

1. The increasing usefulness (specialization) of the thumb and hand, following upright posture.
2. The use of tools.
3. The increasing size and development of the brain.

Nobody knows which of these three is most important, or which came first. Most probably the growth of all three things was very much blended together. If you think about each of the things, you will see what I mean. Unless your hand is more flexible than a paw, and your thumb will work against (or oppose) your fingers, you can't hold a tool very well. But you wouldn't get the idea of using a tool unless you had enough brain to help you see cause and effect. And it is rather hard to see how your hand and brain would develop unless they had something to practice on—like using tools. In Professor Krogman's words, "the hand must become the obedient servant of the eye and the brain." It is the *co-ordination* of these things that counts.

Many other things must have been happening to the bodies of the creatures who were the ancestors of men. Our ancestors had to develop organs of speech. More than that, they had to get the idea of letting *certain sounds* made with these speech organs have *certain meanings*.

All this must have gone very slowly. Probably everything was developing little by little, all together. Men became men very slowly.

WHEN SHALL WE CALL MEN MEN?

What do I mean when I say "men"? People who looked pretty much as we do, and who used different tools to do different things, are men to me. We'll probably never know whether the earliest ones talked or not. They probably had vocal cords, so they could make sounds, but did they know how to make sounds work as symbols to carry meanings? But if the fossil bones look like our skeletons, and if we find tools which we'll agree couldn't have been made by nature or by animals, then I'd say we had traces of *men*.

The fossil bones of the several types of australopithecines in east and south Africa are bound to come into the discussion here. I've already told you that the australopithecines could have stood upright and walked on their two hind legs.. They appear to have lived in open grassland, and their canine teeth are not fang-like but small and of human form. They come from near the base of the Pleistocene or Ice Age, and coarse stone tools have been found with the australopithecine fossils. But there are at least three varieties of australopithecines and they last on until a time equal to that of the second alpine glaciation. They are the best suggestion we have yet as to what the ancestors of men *may* have looked like. They were certainly closer to men than to apes. Although their brain size was no larger than the brain size of modern apes their body size and stature were quite small; hence, relative to their small size, their brains were large. We have not been able to prove without doubt that the australopithecines were *tool-making* creatures, although the number of find-spots with both fossils and tools is increasing. In the case of the 1959 find in Bed I at Olduvai, the *Zinjanthropus* skull (of the australopithecine *Paranthropus* type) appeared both with tools and with broken-up bones of other animals. However, the *Zinjanthropus* bones themselves were not broken up. There are even some "pre-*Zinjanthropus*" finds now awaiting study. The doubt as to whether the australopithecines used tools themselves goes like this—just suppose some man-like creature (whose bones we have not yet found) made the tools and used them to kill and butcher australopithecines? Hence a few experts tend to let australopithecines still hang in limbo as "man-apes."

THE EARLIEST MEN WE KNOW

I'll postpone talking about the tools of early men until the next chapter. The men whose bones were the earliest of the Java lot have been given the name *Meganthropus*. The bones are very fragmentary. We would not understand them very well unless we had the somewhat later Javanese lot—the more commonly known *Pithecanthropus* or "Java man"—against which to refer them for study. One of the less well-known and earliest fragments, a piece of lower jaw and some teeth, rather strongly resembles the lower jaws and teeth of the australopithecine type. Was *Meganthropus* a sort of half-way point between the australopithecines and *Pithecanthropus?* It is still too early to say. We shall need more finds before we can be definite one way or the other.

A find which *may* bear on the problem is the 1960 discovery by Dr. L. S. B. Leakey in Bed II at Olduvai, of a "Chellean" skull. Leakey believes this skull must be of about the same time and type as are the Java and Peking men whom we are about to discuss. The important thing about Leakey's "Chellean" skull is that it comes from exactly the same area where the earlier *Zinjanthropus* types of australopithecines have been turning up. There are certainly tools with this new Olduvai find.

Java man, *Pithecanthropus*, comes from geological beds equal in age to the latter part of the second alpine glaciation; the *Meganthropus* finds refer to beds of the beginning of this glaciation. The first finds of Java man were made in 1891–92 by Dr. Eugene Dubois, a Dutch doctor in the colonial service. Finds have continued to be made. There are now bones enough to account for four skulls. There are also four jaws and some odd teeth and thigh bones. Java man, generally speaking, was about five feet six inches tall, and didn't hold his head very erect. His skull was very thick and heavy and had room for little more than two-thirds as large a brain as we have. He had big teeth and a big jaw and enormous eyebrow ridges.

No tools were found in the geological deposits where bones of Java man appeared. There are some tools in the same general area, but they come a bit later in time. One reason we accept the Java man as man—aside from his general anatomical appearance—is that these tools probably belonged to his near descendants.

Remember that there are several varieties of men in the whole early Java lot, at least two of which are earlier than the *Pithecanthropus*, "Java man." Some of the earlier ones seem to have gone in for bigness, in tooth-size at least. *Meganthropus* is one of these earlier varieties. As we said, he *may* turn out to be a link to the australopithecines, who *may* or *may not* be ancestral to men. *Meganthropus* is best understandable in terms of *Pithecanthropus*, who appeared later in the same general area. *Pithecanthropus* is pretty well understandable from the bones he left us, and also because of his strong resemblance to the fully tool-using cave-dwelling "Peking man," *Sinanthropus*, about whom we shall talk next. The Olduvai "Chellean" man and his tools, of about this same time, would also strengthen the argument. But you can see that the physical anthropologists and prehistoric archeologists still have a lot of work to do on the problem of earliest men.

PEKING MEN AND SOME EARLY WESTERNERS

The earliest known Chinese are called *Sinanthropus*, or "Peking man," because the finds were made near that city. In World War II, the original bones were lost. Fortunately, there is a complete set of casts of the bones, and Chinese scholars have continued to find more bones.

Peking man lived in a cave in a limestone hill, made tools, cracked animal bones to get the marrow out, and used fire.

Peking man was not quite as tall as Java man but he probably stood straighter. His skull looked very much like that of the Java skull except that it had room for a slightly larger brain. His face was less brutish than was Java man's face, but this isn't saying much.

Peking man dates from early in the interglacial period following the second alpine glaciation. He probably lived close to 350,000 years ago. There are several finds to account for in Europe by about this time, and one from northwest Africa (Ternafine). The very large jawbone found near Heidelberg in Germany is doubtless even earlier than Peking man. The beds where it was found are of second alpine glacial times, and recently some tools have been said to have come from the same beds. There is not much I need tell you about the Heidelberg jaw save that it seems certainly to have belonged to an early man, and that it is very big.

Another find in Germany was made at Steinheim. It consists of the fragmentary skull of a man. It is very important because of its relative completeness, but it has not yet been fully studied. The bone is thick, but the back of the head is neither very low nor primitive, and the face is also not primitive. The forehead does, however, have big ridges over the eyes. The more fragmentary skull from Swanscombe in England (p. 11) has been much more carefully studied. Only the top and back of that skull have been found. Since the skull rounds up nicely, it has been assumed that the face and forehead must have been quite "modern." Careful comparison with the Steinheim skull shows that this was not necessarily so. This is important, as we shall see, for it bears on the question of how early truly "modern" man appeared.

Recently two fragmentary jaws were found at Ternafine in Algeria, northwest Africa. They look like the jaws of Peking man. Tools were found with them. No jaws have been found at Steinheim or Swanscombe, but the time is the same; one wonders if these people had jaws like those at Ternafine.

WHAT HAPPENED TO JAVA AND PEKING MEN

Professor Weidenreich thought that there were at least a dozen ways in which the Peking man resembled the modern Mongoloids. More recent thought on the matter would not suggest racial differences this early.

Several later fossil men have been found in the Java-Australian area. The best known of these is the so-called Solo man. There are some finds from Australia itself which we now know to be quite late. Possibly we may assume a line of evolution from Java man down to the modern Australian natives. During parts of the Ice Age there was a land bridge all the way from Java to Australia.

TWO ENGLISHMEN WHO WEREN'T OLD

The older textbooks contain descriptions of two English finds which were thought to be very old. These were called Piltdown (*Eoanthropus dawsoni*) and Galley Hill. The skulls were very modern in appearance. In 1948–49, British scientists began making chemical tests which proved that neither of these finds is very old. It is now known that both "Piltdown man" and the tools which were said to have been found with him were part of an elaborate fake!

TYPICAL "CAVE MEN"

The next men we have to talk about are all members of a related group. This is the Neanderthal group. "Neanderthal man" himself was found in the Neander Valley, near

Düsseldorf, Germany, in 1856. He was the first human fossil to be recognized as such.

Some of us think that the neanderthaloids proper are only those people of western Europe who didn't get out before the beginning of the last great glaciation, and who found them-

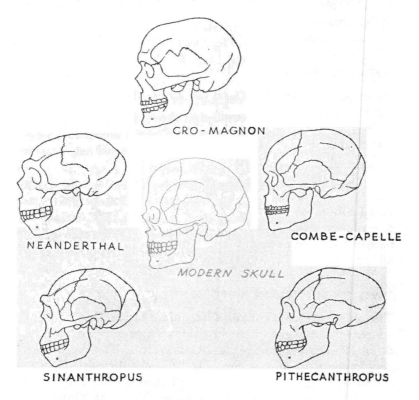

PRINCIPAL KNOWN TYPES OF FOSSIL MEN

selves hemmed in by the glaciers in the Alps and northern Europe. Being hemmed in, they intermarried a bit too much and developed into a special type. Professor F. Clark Howell sees it this way. In Europe, the earliest trace of men we now know is the Heidelberg jaw. Evolution continued in Europe, from Heidelberg through the Swanscombe and Steinheim types to a group of pre-neanderthaloids. There are traces of these pre-neanderthaloids pretty much throughout Europe during the third interglacial period—say 100,000 years ago. The pre-neanderthaloids are represented by such finds as the ones at Ehringsdorf in Germany and Saccopastore in Italy. I won't describe them for you, since they are simply less extreme than the neanderthaloids proper—about half way between the Steinheim and the classic Neanderthal people.

Professor Howell believes that the pre-neanderthaloids who happened to get caught in the pocket of the southwest corner of Europe at the onset of the last great glaciation became the classic Neanderthalers. Out in the Near East, Howell thinks, it is possible to see traces of people evolving from the pre-neanderthaloid type toward that of fully modern man. Certainly, we don't see such extreme cases of "neanderthaloidism" outside of western Europe.

There are at least a dozen good examples in the main or classic Neanderthal group in Europe. They date to just before and in the earlier part of the last great glaciation (85,000 to 40,000 years ago). Many of the finds have been made in caves. The "cave men" the movies and the cartoonists show you are probably meant to be Neanderthalers. I'm not at all sure they dragged their women by the hair, however; the women were probably pretty tough, too!.

Neanderthal men had large bony heads, but plenty of room for brains. Some had brain cases even larger than the average for modern man. Their faces were heavy, and they had eyebrow ridges of bone, but the ridges were not as big as those of Java man. Their foreheads were very low, and they didn't have much chin. They were about five feet three inches tall, but were heavy and barrel-chested.

One important thing about the Neanderthal group is that there is a fair number of them to study. Just as important is the fact that we know quite a bit about how they lived, and about some of the tools they made.

OTHER MEN CONTEMPORARY WITH
THE NEANDERTHALOIDS

We have seen that the neanderthaloids seem to be a specialization in a corner of Europe. What was going on elsewhere?

We think that the pre-neanderthaloid type was a generally widespread form of men. From this type evolved other more or less extreme although generally related men. The Solo finds in Java form one such case. Another was the Rhodesian man of Africa, and the more recent Hopefield finds show more of the general Rhodesian type. It is more confusing than it needs to be if these cases outside western Europe are called neanderthaloids. They lived during the same approximate time range but they were all somewhat different-looking people.

EARLY MODERN MEN

How early is modern man (*Homo sapiens*), the "wise man"? Some people have thought that he was very early, a few still think so. Piltdown and Galley Hill, which were quite modern in anatomical appearance and *supposedly* very early in date, were the best "evidence" for very early modern men. Now that Piltdown has been liquidated and Galley Hill is known to be very late, what is left of the idea?

The backs of the skulls of the Swanscombe and Steinheim finds look rather modern. Unless you pay attention to the face and forehead of the Steinheim find—which not many people have—and perhaps also consider the Ternafine jaws, you might come to the conclusion that the crown of the Swanscombe head was that of a modern-like man.

Two more skulls, again without faces, are available from a French cave site, Fontéchevade. They come from the time of the last great interglacial, as did the pre-neanderthaloids. The crowns of the Fontéchevade skulls also look quite modern. There is a bit of the forehead preserved on one of these skulls and the brow-ridge is not heavy. Nevertheless, there is a suggestion that the bones belonged to an immature individual. In this case, his (or even more so, if *her*) brow-ridges would have been weak anyway. The case for the Fontéchevade fossils, as modern type men, is little stronger than that for Swanscombe, although Professor Vallois believes it a good case.

It seems to add up to the fact that there were people living in Europe—before the classic neanderthaloids—who looked more modern, in some features, than the classic western neanderthaloids did. Our best suggestion of what men looked like—just before they became fully modern—comes from a cave on Mount Carmel in Palestine.

THE FIRST MODERNS

Professor T. D. McCown and the late Sir Arthur Keith, who studied the Mount Carmel bones, figured out that one of the two groups involved was as much as 70 per cent modern. There were, in fact, two groups or varieties of men in the Mount Carmel caves and in at least two other Palestinian caves of about the same time. The time would be about that of the onset of colder weather, when the last glaciation was beginning in the north—say 75,000 years ago.

The modern group came from only one Mount Carmel cave, Mugharet es-Skhul ("cave of the kids"). The other group, from several caves, had bones of men of the type we've been calling pre-neanderthaloid which we noted were widespread in Europe and beyond. The tools which came with each of these finds were generally similar, and McCown and Keith, and other scholars since their study, have tended to assume that both the Skhul group and the pre-neanderthaloid group came from exactly the same time. The conclusion was quite natural: here was a population of men in the act of evolving in two different directions. But the time may not be exactly the same. It is very difficult to be precise, within say 10,000 years, for a time some 75,000 years ago. If the Skhul men are in fact later than the pre-neanderthaloid group of Palestine, as some of us think, then they show how relatively modern some men were—men who lived at the same time as the classic Neanderthalers of the European pocket.

Southwestern Asia is an area of interest concerning the question of where early modern man developed. The more modern Skhul and Kafzeh finds contrast with those of Tabun, other Palestinian finds, and an important new group from Shanidar in Kurdistan. These latter are of more generalized neanderthaloid type, as is a newly reported skull from Greece.

Soon after the first extremely cold phase of the last glaciation, we begin to get a number of bones of completely

modern men in Europe. We also get great numbers of the
tools they made, and their living places in caves. Completely
modern skeletons begin turning up in caves dating back to
toward 40,000 years ago. The time is about that of the
beginning of the second phase of the last glaciation. These
skeletons belonged to people no different from many people
we see today. Like people today, not everybody looked alike.
(The positions of the more important fossil men of later
Europe are shown in the chart on page 72.)

DIFFERENCES IN THE EARLY MODERNS

The main early European moderns have been divided into
two groups, the Cro-Magnon group and the Combe Capelle-
Brünn group. Cro-Magnon people were tall and big-boned,
with large, long, and rugged heads. They must have been
built like many present-day Scandinavians. The Combe
Capelle-Brünn people were shorter; they had narrow heads
and faces, and big eyebrow-ridges. Of course we don't find
the skin or hair of these people. But there is little doubt they
were Caucasoids ("Whites").

Another important find came in the Italian Riviera, near
Monte Carlo. Here, in a cave near Grimaldi, there was
a grave containing a woman and a young boy, buried together.
The two skeletons were first called "Negroid" because some
features of their bones were thought to resemble certain
features of modern African Negro bones. But more recently,
Professor E. A. Hooton and other experts questioned the use
of the word "Negroid" in describing the Grimaldi skeletons.
It is true that nothing is known of the skin color, hair form,
or any other fleshy feature of the Grimaldi people, so that
the word "Negroid" in its usual meaning is not proper here.
It is also not clear whether the features of the bones claimed
to be "Negroid" are really so at all.

From a place called Wadjak, in Java, we have "proto-
Australoid" skulls which closely resemble those of modern
Australian natives. Some of the skulls found in South Africa,
especially the Boskop skull, look like those of modern Bushmen,
but are much bigger. The ancestors of the Bushmen seem to
have once been very widespread south of the Sahara Desert.

True African Negroes were forest people who apparently expanded out of the west central African area only in the last several thousand years. Although dark in skin color, neither the Australians nor the Bushmen are Negroes; neither the Wadjak nor the Boskop skulls are "Negroid."

As we've already mentioned, Professor Weidenreich believed that Peking man was already on the way to becoming a Mongoloid. Anyway, the Mongoloids would seem to have been present by the time of the "Upper Cave" at Choukoutien, the *Sinanthropus* find-spot, but well after Peking man in time.

WHAT THE DIFFERENCES MEAN

What does all this difference mean? It means that, at one moment in time, within each different area, men tended to look somewhat alike. From area to area, men tended to look somewhat different, just as they do today. This is all quite natural. People *tended* to mate near home; in the anthropological jargon, they made up geographically localized breeding populations. The simple continental division of "stocks"—black = Africa, yellow = Asia, white = Europe—is too simple a picture to fit the facts. People became accustomed to life in some particular area within a continent (we might call it a "natural area"). As they went on living there, they evolved towards some particular physical variety. It would, of course, have been difficult to draw a clear boundary between two adjacent areas. There must always have been some mating across the boundaries in every case. One thing human beings don't do, and never have done, is to mate for "purity." It is self-righteous nonsense when we try to kid ourselves into thinking that they do.

I am not going to struggle with the whole business of modern stocks and races. This is a book about prehistoric men, not recent historic or modern men. My physical anthropologist friends have been very patient in helping me to write and rewrite this chapter—I am not going to break their patience completely. Races are their business, not mine, and they must do the writing about races. I shall, however, give two modern definitions of race, and then make one comment.

Dr. William C. Boyd, professor of Immunochemistry, School of Medicine, Boston University: "We may define a human race as a population which differs significantly from other human populations in regard to the frequency of one or more of the genes it possesses."

Professor Sherwood L. Washburn, professor of Physical Anthropology, Department of Anthropology, the University of California: "A 'race' is a group of genetically similar populations, and races intergrade because there are always intermediate populations."

My comment is that the ideas involved here are all biological; they concern groups, *not* individuals. Boyd and Washburn may differ a bit on what they want to consider a "population," but a population is a group nevertheless, and genetics is biology to the hilt. Now a lot of people still think of race in terms of how people dress or fix their food or of other habits or customs they have. The next step is to talk about racial "purity" or "superiority." None of this has anything whatever to do with race proper, which is a matter of the biology of groups.

Incidentally, I'm told that if man very carefully *controls* the breeding of certain animals over generations—dogs, cattle, chickens—he might achieve a "pure" race of animals. But he doesn't do it. Some unfortunate genetic trait soon turns up, so this has just as carefully to be bred out again, and so on.

SUMMARY OF PRESENT KNOWLEDGE
OF FOSSIL MEN

At this moment, the evidence bearing on human evolution appears to subdivide into three stages:

1. An australopithecine stage, back over a million years ago, with several varieties of forms and with crude stone tools associated with at least some of them.

2. An early human (*Homo erectus*) stage, beginning at least with the Java, Olduvai "Chellean" and Peking men at perhaps a half million years ago and lasting down through the Heidelberg, Ternafine, Steinheim, and Swanscombe finds to

about 40,000 years ago with the classic Neanderthalers and their contemporaries.

3. Beginning about 40,000 years ago, the first traces of fully modern skeletons in Europe, which seem to have been anticipated in southwestern Asia by the pre-modern types such as Skhul.

There seems to be an increasing likelihood that the beings of the first stage will be accepted as "men." There is no question that we are dealing with tool-making humans in the second and third stages.

You will note a quickening of pace as the stages develop. Men were learning ever better ways to adjust to the variety and to the changes in their environment. The fossil bones of their bodies show these adjustments, but the pace of the change is also amply demonstrated by the tools they made. That is the part of the story which the prehistoric archeologist must tell.

Cultural BEGINNINGS

Men, unlike the lower animals, are made up of much more than flesh and blood and bones; for men have "culture."

WHAT IS CULTURE?

"Culture" is a word with many meanings. The doctors speak of making a "culture" of a certain kind of bacteria, and ants are said to have a "culture." Then there is the Emily Post kind of "culture"—you say a person is "cultured," or that he isn't, depending on such things as whether or not he eats peas with his knife.

The anthropologists use the word too, and argue heatedly over its finer meanings; but they all agree that every human being is part of or has some kind of culture. Each particular human group has a particular culture; that is one of the ways in which we can tell one group of men from another. In this sense, a *culture* means the way the members of a group of people think and believe and live, the tools they make, and the way they do things. Professor Robert Redfield said that a culture is an organized or formalized body of conventional understandings. "Conventional understandings" means the whole set of rules, beliefs, and standards which a group of people lives by. These understandings show themselves in art, and in the other things a people may make and do. The understandings continue to last, through tradition, from one generation to another. They are what really characterize different human groups.

SOME CHARACTERISTICS OF CULTURE

A culture lasts, although individual men in the group die off. On the other hand, a culture changes as the different conventions and understandings change. You could almost say that a culture lives in the minds of the men who have it. But people are not born with it; they get it as they grow up. Suppose a day-old Hungarian baby is adopted by a family in Oshkosh, Wisconsin, and the child is not told that he is Hungarian. He will grow up with no more idea of Hungarian culture than anyone else in Oshkosh.

So when I speak of ancient Egyptian culture, I mean the whole body of understandings and beliefs and knowledge possessed by the ancient Egyptians. I mean their beliefs as to why grain grew, as well as their ability to make tools with which to reap the grain. I mean their beliefs about life after death. What I am thinking about as culture is a thing which lasted in time. If any one Egyptian, even the Pharaoh, died, it didn't affect the Egyptian culture of that particular moment.

PREHISTORIC CULTURES

For that long period of man's history that is all prehistory, we have no written descriptions of cultures. We find only the tools men made, the places where they lived, the graves in which they buried their dead. Fortunately for us, these tools and living places and graves all tell us something about the ways these men lived and the things they believed. But the story we learn of the very early cultures must be only a very small part of the whole, for we find so few things. The rest of the story is gone forever. We have to do what we can with what we find.

For all of the time up to about 75,000 years ago, which was the time of the classic European Neanderthal group of men, we have found few cave-dwelling places of very early prehistoric men. First, there is the fallen-in cave where

Peking man was found, near Peking. Then there are two or three other *early*, but not *very early*, possibilities. The finds at the base of the French cave of Fontéchevade, those in one of the Makapan caves in South Africa, and several open sites such as Dr. L. S. B. Leakey's Olorgesailie in Kenya doubtless all lie earlier than the time of the main European Neanderthal group, but none are so early as the Peking finds.

You can see that we know very little about the home life of earlier prehistoric men. We find different kinds of early stone tools, but we can't even be really sure which tools may have been used together.

WHY LITTLE HAS LASTED FROM EARLY TIMES

Except for the rare find-spots mentioned above, all our very early finds come from geological deposits, or from the wind-blown surfaces of deserts. Here is what the business of geological deposits really means. Let us say that a group of people was living in England about 300,000 years ago. They made the tools they needed, lived in some sort of camp, almost certainly built fires, and perhaps buried their dead. While the climate was still warm, many generations may have lived in the same place, hunting, and gathering nuts and berries; but after some few thousand years, the weather began very gradually to grow colder. These early Englishmen would not have known that a glacier was forming over northern Europe. They would only have noticed that the animals they hunted seemed to be moving south, and that the berries grew larger toward the south. So they would have moved south, too.

The camp site they left is the place we archeologists would really have liked to find. All of the different tools the people used would have been there together—many broken, some whole. The graves, and traces of fire, and the tools would have been there. But the glacier got there first! The front of this enormous sheet of ice moved down over the country, crushing and breaking and plowing up everything, like a gigantic bulldozer. You can see what happened to our camp site.

Everything the glacier couldn't break, it pushed along in front of it or plowed beneath it. Rocks were ground to gravel, and soil was caught into the ice, which afterwards melted and ran off as muddy water. Hard tools of flint sometimes remained whole. Human bones weren't so hard; it's a wonder *any* of them lasted. Gushing streams of melt water flushed out the debris from underneath the glacier, and water flowed off the surface and through great crevasses. The hard materials these waters carried were even more rolled and ground up. Finally, such materials were dropped by the rushing waters as gravels, miles from the front of the glacier. At last the glacier reached its greatest extent; then it melted backward toward the north. Debris held in the ice was dropped where the ice melted, or was flushed off by more melt water. When the glacier, leaving the land, had withdrawn to the sea, great hunks of ice were broken off as icebergs. These icebergs probably dropped the materials held in their ice wherever they floated and melted. There must be many tools and fragmentary bones of prehistoric men on the bottom of the Atlantic Ocean and the North Sea.

Remember, too, that these glaciers came and went at least three or four times during the Ice Age. Then you will realize why the earlier things we find are all mixed up. Stone tools from one camp site got mixed up with stone tools from many other camp sites—tools which may have been made tens of thousands or more years apart. The glaciers mixed them all up, and so we often cannot say which particular sets of tools belonged together in the first place.

"EOLITHS"

But what sort of tools do we find earliest? For almost a century, people have been picking up odd bits of flint and other stone in the oldest Ice Age gravels in England and France. It is now thought these odd bits of stone weren't actually worked by prehistoric men. The stones were given a name, *eoliths*, or "dawn stones." You can see them in many museums; but you can be pretty sure that very few of them were actually fashioned by men.

It is impossible to pick out "eoliths" that seem to be made in any one *tradition*. By "tradition" I mean a set of habits for making one kind of tool for some particular job. No two "eoliths" look very much alike; tools made as part of some one tradition all look much alike. Now it's easy to suppose that the very earliest prehistoric men picked up and used almost any sort of stone. This wouldn't be surprising; you and I do it when we go camping. In other words, some of these "eoliths" may actually have been used by prehistoric men. They must have used anything that might be handy when they needed it. We could have figured that out without the "eoliths."

THE ROAD TO STANDARDIZATION

Reasoning from what we know or can easily imagine, there should have been three major steps in the prehistory of tool-making. The first step would have been simple *utilization* of what was at hand. This is the step into which the "eoliths" would fall. The second step would have been *fashioning*—the haphazard preparation of a tool when there was a need for it. Probably many of the earlier pebble tools, which I shall describe next, fall into this group. The third step would have been *standardization*. Here, men began to make tools according to certain set traditions. Counting the better-made pebble tools, there are four such traditions or sets of habits for the production of stone tools in earliest prehistoric times. Toward the end of the Pleistocene, a fifth tradition appears.

PEBBLE TOOLS

At the beginning of the last chapter I said there were tools from very early geological beds. The earliest bones of men have not yet been found in quite such early beds although the Olduvai, Sterkfontein and Swartkrans australopithecine finds approach this early date. The earliest tools come from Africa. They date back at least to the time of the first great alpine glaciation and are over a million years old. The earliest ones are made of split pebbles, about the size of your fist or a bit bigger. They go under the name of pebble tools. There are many natural exposures of early Pleistocene geological beds in Africa, and the prehistoric archeologists of south and central Africa have concentrated on searching for early tools.

Other finds of early pebble tools have recently been made in Algeria and Morocco. There are probably early pebble tools to be found in areas of the Old World besides Africa; in fact, some prehistorians already have identified a few in Europe and the Near East.

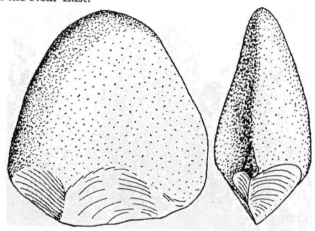

SOUTH AFRICAN PEBBLE TOOL

Since the forms and the distinct ways of making the earlier pebble tools had not yet sufficiently jelled into a set tradition, they are difficult for us to recognize. It is not so difficult, however, if there are great numbers of "possibles" available, A little later in time the tradition becomes more clearly set. and pebble tools are easier to recognize. So far, really large collections of pebble tools have only been found and examined in Africa.

CORE-BIFACE TOOLS

The next tradition we'll look at is the *core* or biface one. The tools are large pear-shaped pieces of stone trimmed flat on the two opposite sides or "faces." Hence "biface" has been used to describe these tools. The front view is like that of a pear with a rather pointed top, and the back view looks almost exactly the same. Look at them side on, and you can see that the front and back faces are the same and have been trimmed to a thin tip. The real purpose in trimming down the two faces was to get a good cutting edge all around. You can see all this in the illustration.

We have very little idea of the way in which these core-bifaces were used. They have been called "hand axes," but

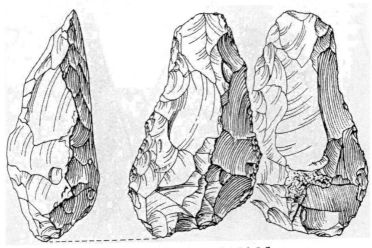

ABBEVILLIAN   BIFACE

this probably gives the wrong idea, for an ax, to us, is not a pointed tool. All of these early tools must have been used for a number of jobs—chopping, scraping, cutting, hitting, picking, and prying. Since the core-bifaces tend to be pointed, it seems likely that they were used for hitting, picking, and prying. But they have rough cutting edges, so they could have been used for chopping, scraping, and cutting.

FLAKE TOOLS

The third tradition is the *flake* tradition. The idea was to get a tool with a good cutting edge by simply knocking a nice large flake off a big block of stone. You had to break off the flake in such a way that it was broad and thin, and also had a good sharp cutting edge. Once you really got on to the trick of doing it, this was probably a simpler way to make a good cutting tool than preparing a biface. You have to know how, though; I've tried it and have mashed my fingers more than once.

The flake tools look as if they were meant mainly for chopping, scraping, and cutting jobs. When one made a flake

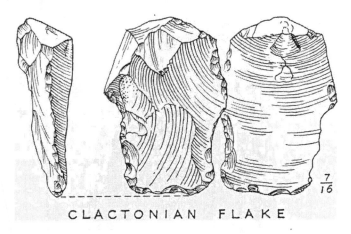

CLACTONIAN   FLAKE

the idea seems to have been to produce a broad, sharp, ıg edge.

ıe core-biface and the flake traditions were spread, arliest times, over much of Europe, Africa, and western The map on page 52 shows the general area. Over ɔf this great region there was flint. Both of these ıs seem well adapted to flint, although good core- and flakes were made from other kinds of stone, ʋ in Africa south of the Sahara.

RS AND ADZE-LIKE TOOLS

h early tradition is found in southern and eastern northwestern India through Java and Burma into ther Maringer recently reported an early group of ɔan, which most resemble those of Java, called The prehistoric men in this general area mostly and tuff and even petrified wood for their stone ıstration, p. 46).

·th early tradition is called the *chopper-chopping* It probably has its earliest roots in the pebble of African type. There are several kinds of

The
f an

kit of
ve in-

tools in this tradition, but all differ from the western core-bifaces and flakes. There are broad, heavy scrapers or cleavers, and tools with an adze-like cutting edge. These last-named tools are called "hand adzes," just as the core-

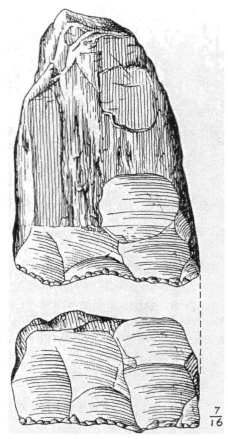

ANYATHIAN
ADZE-LIKE TOOL

bifaces of the west have often been called "hand axes." section of an adze cutting edge is $\angle$ shaped; the section ax is $<$ shaped.

There are also pointed pebble tools. Thus the tool these early south and east Asiatic peoples seems to ha cluded tools for doing as many different jobs as did the tools of the Western traditions. Dr. H. L. Movius has emphasized that the tools which were found in the Peking cave with Peking man belong to the chopper tool tradition. With the exception of the australopithecine coarse pebble tools, the Peking chopper tools and the Olduvai "Chellean" core-bifaces are the earliest cases of man-and-tools in one find-spot.

DIFFERENCES WITHIN THE TOOL-MAKING TRADITIONS

The latter three great traditions in the manufacture of stone tools—and the less clear-cut pebble tools before them—are all we have to show of the cultures of the men of those times. Changes happened in each of the traditions. As time went on, the tools in each tradition were better made. There could also be slight regional differences in the tools within one tradition. Thus, tools with small differences, but all belonging to one tradition, can be given special group (facies) names.

This naming of special groups has been going on for some time. Here are some of these names, since you may see them used in museum displays of flint tools, or in books. Within each tradition of tool-making (save the chopper tools), the earliest tool type is at the bottom of the list, just as it appears in the lowest beds of a geological stratification.[1]

Chopper tool (all about equally early):
Anyathian (Burma)
Choukoutienian (China)
Patjitanian (Java)
Soan (India)

Flake:
"Typical Mousterian"
Levalloiso-Mousterian
Levalloisian
Tayacian
Clactonian

[1] Archeologists usually make their charts and lists with the earliest materials at the bottom and the latest on top, since this is the way they find them in the ground.

Core-biface:
   Some blended elements in "Mousterian"
   Micoquian (=Acheulean 6 and 7)
   Acheulean
   Abbevillian (once called "Chellean")

Pebble tool:
   Oldowan
   Ain Hanech
   pre-Stellenbosch
   Kafuan

The core-biface and the flake traditions appear in the chart (p. 65).

The early archeologists had many of the tool groups named before they ever realized that there were broader tool preparation traditions. This was understandable, for in dealing with the mixture of things that come out of glacial gravels the easiest thing to do first is to isolate individual types of tools into groups. First you put a bushel-basketful of tools on a table and begin matching up types. Then you give names to the groups of each type. The groups and the types are really matters of the archeologists' choice; in real life, they were probably less exact than the archeologists' lists of them. We now know pretty well in which of the early traditions the various early groups belong.

THE MEANING OF THE DIFFERENT TRADITIONS

What do the traditions really mean? I see them as the standardization of ways to make tools for particular jobs. We may not know exactly what job the maker of a particular core-biface or flake tool had in mind. We can easily see, however, that he already enjoyed a know-how, a set of persistent habits of tool preparation, which would always give him the same type of tool when he wanted to make it. Therefore, the traditions show us that persistent habits already existed for the preparation of one type of tool or another.

This tells us that one of the characteristic aspects of human culture was already present. There must have been, in the minds of these early men, a notion of the ideal type of tool for a particular job.   Furthermore, since we find so many thousands upon thousands of tools of one type or another, the notion of the ideal types of tools *and* the know-how for the making of each type must have been held in common by many men.   The notions of the ideal types and the know-how for their production must have been passed on from one generation to another.

I could even guess that the notions of the ideal type of one or the other of these tools stood out in the minds of men of those times somewhat like a symbol of "perfect tool for good job."   If this were so—remember it's only a wild guess of mine—then men were already symbol users.   Now let's go on a further step to the fact that the words men speak are simply sounds, each different sound being a symbol for a different meaning.   If standardized tool-making suggests symbol-making, is it also possible that crude word-symbols were also being made?   I suppose that it is not impossible.

There may, of course, be a real question whether tool-utilizing creatures—our first step, on page 42—were actually men.   Other animals utilize things at hand as tools.   The tool-fashioning creature of our second step is more suggestive, although we may not yet feel sure that many of the earlier pebble tools were man-made products.   But with the step to standardization and the appearance of the traditions, I believe we must surely be dealing with the traces of culture-bearing *men*.   The "conventional understandings" which Professor Redfield's definition of culture suggests are now evidenced for us in the persistent habits for the preparation of stone tools. Were we able to see the other things these prehistoric men must have made—in materials no longer preserved for the archeologist to find—I believe there would be clear signs of further conventional understandings.   The men may have been physically primitive and pretty shaggy in appearance, but I think we must surely call them men.

AN OLDER INTERPRETATION OF THE
    WESTERN TRADITIONS

In the last chapter, I told you that many of the older archeologists and human paleontologists used to think that modern man was very old. The supposed ages of Piltdown and Galley Hill were given as evidence of the great age of anatomically modern man, and some interpretations of the Swanscombe and Fontéchevade fossils were taken to support this view. The conclusion was that there were two separate and parallel lines or "phyla" of men already present well back in the Pleistocene. The first, the more primitive or "paleoanthropic" line, was said to include Heidelberg, the proto-neanderthaloids and classic Neanderthal. The more anatomically modern or "neanthropic" line was thought to consist of Piltdown and the others mentioned above. The Neanderthaler or paleoanthropic line was thought to have become extinct after the first phase of the last great glaciation. Of course, the modern or neanthropic line was believed to have persisted into the present, as the basis for the world's population today. But with Piltdown liquidated, Galley Hill known to be very late, and Swanscombe and Fontéchevade otherwise interpreted, there is little left of the so-called parallel phyla theory.

While the theory was in vogue, however, and as long as the European archeological evidence was looked at in one short-sighted way, the archeological materials *seemed* to fit the parallel phyla theory. It was simply necessary to believe that the flake tools were made only by the paleoanthropic Neanderthaler line, and that the more handsome core-biface tools were the product of the neanthropic modern-man line.

Remember that *almost* all of the early prehistoric European tools came only from the redeposited gravel beds. This means that the tools were not normally found in the remains of camp-sites or work shops where they had actually been dropped by the men who made and used them. The tools came, rather, from the secondary hodge-podge of the glacial gravels. I tried to give you a picture of the bulldozing action of glaciers (p. 40) and of the erosion and weathering that were side-effects of a glacially conditioned climate on the earth's surface. As we said above, if one simply plucks tools out of the redeposited gravels, his natural tendency is to "type" the tools by groups, and to think that the groups stand for something *on their own.*

In 1906, M. Victor Commont actually made a rare find of what seems to have been a kind of workshop site, on a terrace above the Somme River in France. Here, Commont realized, flake tools appeared clearly in direct association with core-biface tools. Few prehistorians paid attention to Commont or his site, however. It was easier to believe that flake tools represented a distinct "culture" and that this "culture" was that of the Neanderthaler or paleoanthropic line, and that the core-bifaces stood for another "culture" which was that of the supposed early modern or neanthropic line. Of course, I am obviously skipping many details here. Some later sites with Neanderthal fossils do seem to have only flake tools, but other such sites have both types of tools. The flake tools which appeared *with* the core-bifaces in the Swanscombe gravels were never made much of, although it was embarrassing for the parallel phyla people that Fontéchevade ran heavily to flake tools. All in all, the parallel phyla theory flourished because it seemed so neat and easy to understand.

TRADITIONS ARE TOOL-MAKING HABITS, NOT CULTURES

In case you think I simply enjoy beating a dead horse, look in any standard book on prehistory written twenty (or even ten) years ago, or in most encyclopedias. You'll find that each of the individual tool types, of the West, at least, was supposed to represent a "culture." The "cultures" were believed to correspond to parallel lines of human evolution.

In 1937, Mr. Harper Kelley strongly re-emphasized the importance of Commont's workshop site and the presence of flake tools with core-bifaces. Next followed Dr. Movius' clear delineation of the chopper-chopping tool tradition of the Far East. This spoiled the nice symmetry of the flake-tool= paleoanthropic, core-biface=neanthropic equations. The supposed symmetry was further broken by (a) increased understanding of the early African pebble tools, and (b) by the large numbers of both core-biface and flake tools occurring together in open-air sites such as Olorgesailie in Kenya and Torralba in Spain. Then came increasing understanding of

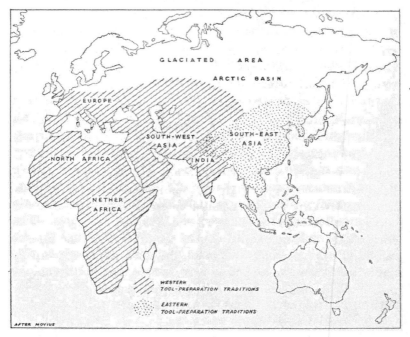

DISTRIBUTION OF TOOL-PREPARATION TRADITIONS
Time approximately 100,000 years ago

the importance of the pebble tools in Africa, and the location
of several more workshop sites there, especially at Olorgesailie
in Kenya.   Finally came the liquidation of Piltdown and the
deflation of Galley Hill's date.   So it is at last possible to picture an individual prehistoric man making a flake tool to do
one job and a core-biface tool to do another.   Commont
showed us this picture in 1906, but few believed him.

There are certainly a few cases in which flake tools did
appear with few or no core-bifaces.   The Clactonian flake-
tool group in western Europe is such a case.   Another good,
but certainly later case is that of the cave on Mount Carmel in
Palestine, where the blended pre-neanderthaloid, 70 per cent
modern-type skulls were found.   Here, in the same level with
the skulls, were 9,784 flint tools.   Of these, only three—
doubtless strays—were core-bifaces; all the rest were flake
tools or flake chips.   We noted above how the Fontéchevade
cave ran to flake tools.   The only conclusion I would draw

from this is that times and circumstances did exist in which prehistoric men needed only flake tools. So they only made flake tools for those particular times and circumstances.

LIFE IN EARLIEST TIMES

What do we actually know of life in these earliest times? In the glacial gravels, or in the terrace gravels of rivers once swollen by floods of melt water or heavy rains, or on the windswept deserts, we find stone tools. The earliest and coarsest of these are the pebble tools. The australopithecines probably give us a good hint of what the men who made them looked like. Then begin the more formal tool-preparation traditions of the west—the core-bifaces and the flake tools—and the chopper-chopping tool series of the farther east. There is an occasional roughly worked piece of bone. From the gravels which yield Clactonian flakes in England comes the fire-hardened point of a wooden spear. There are also the chance finds of the fossil human bones themselves, of which we spoke in the last chapter. Aside from the cave of Peking man, none of the tools of the earliest firm traditions have been found in caves. Open air or "workshop" sites which do not seem to have been disturbed later by some geological agency are very rare.

The chart on page 65 shows graphically what the situation in west-central Europe seems to have been. It is not yet certain whether there were pebble tools there, although Dr. A. Rust claims some from Heidelberg. The Fontéchevade cave comes into the picture about 100,000 years ago or more. But for the earlier hundreds of thousands of years—below the red-dotted line on the chart—the tools we have found, until very recently, have come almost entirely from the haphazard mixture within the geological contexts.

The stone tools of each of the earlier traditions are the simplest kinds of all-purpose tools. Almost any one of them could be used for hacking, chopping, cutting, and scraping; so the men who used them must have been living in a rough and ready sort of way. They found or hunted their food wherever they could. In the anthropological jargon, they were "food-gatherers," pure and simple.

Because of the mixture in the gravels and in the materials they carried, we can't be sure which animals these men hunted. Bones of the larger animals turn up in the gravels, but they could just as well belong to the animals who hunted the men, rather than the other way about. We don't know. This is why camp sites like Commont's and Olorgesailie in Kenya are so important when we do find them. Fortunately, now that prehistorians have come to recognize this importance, more and more are being discovered. The animal bones at Olorgesailie belonged to various mammals of extremely large size. Probably they were taken in pit-traps, but there are a number of groups of three round stones on the site which suggest that the people used bolas. The South American Indians used three-ball bolas, with the stones in separate leather bags connected by thongs. These were whirled and· then thrown through the air so as to entangle the feet of a fleeing animal.

Several years ago, after excavating another important open air site at Isimila in Tanganyika, Professor F. Clark Howell began work at two large European open-air sites, Torralba and Ambrona, north of Madrid in Spain. Each of these sites yielded the bones of many fossil animals and also thousands of core-bifaces, flakes, and choppers. But Howell's reconstruction of the food-getting habits of the peoples of this period certainly suggests that the word "hunting" is too dignified for what they did; "scavenging" would be much nearer the mark.

During a great part of this time the climate was warm and pleasant. The second interglacial period (the time between the second and third great alpine glaciations) lasted a long time, and during much of this time the climate may have been even better than ours is now. We don't know that earlier prehistoric men in Europe or Africa lived in caves. They may not have needed to; much of the weather may have been so nice that they lived in the open and they didn't wear clothes.

WHAT THE PEKING CAVE-FINDS TELL US

The one early cave dwelling we have found is that of Peking man, in China. Peking man had fire. He probably cooked his meat, or used the fire to keep dangerous animals away from his den. In the cave were bones of dangerous animals, members of the wolf, bear, and cat families. Some of the cat bones belonged to beasts larger than tigers. There were also bones of other wild animals: buffalo, camel, deer, elephants, horses, sheep, and even ostriches. Seventy per cent of the animals Peking man killed were fallow deer. It's much too cold and dry in north China for all these animals to live there today. So this list helps us know that the weather was reasonably warm, and that there was enough rain to grow grass for the grazing animals.

Peking man also seems to have eaten plant food, for there are hackberry seeds in the debris of the cave. His tools were made of sandstone and quartz and sometimes of a rather bad flint. As we've already seen, they belong in the chopper-tool tradition. It seems fairly clear that some of the edges were chipped by right-handed people. There are also many split pieces of heavy bone. Peking man probably split them so he could eat the bone marrow; he may have used them as tools.

Many of these split bones were the bones of Peking men. Each one of the skulls had already had the base broken out of it. In no case were any of the bones resting together in their natural relation to one another. There is nothing like a burial; all of the bones are scattered. Now it's true that animals could have scattered bodies that were not cared for or buried. But splitting bones lengthwise and carefully removing the base of a skull call for both the tools and the people to use them. It's pretty clear who the people were. Peking man was a cannibal.

––––––––––

This rounds out about all we can say of the life and times of early prehistoric men. In those days life was rough. You evidently had to watch out not only for dangerous animals but also for your fellow men. You ate whatever you could catch or find growing. But you had sense enough to build fires, and you had already formed certain habits for making the kinds of stone tools you needed. That's about all we know. But I think we'll have to admit that cultural beginnings had been made, and that these early people were really *men*.

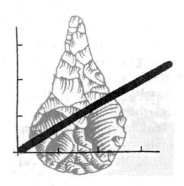

MORE EVIDENCE of Culture

While the dating is not yet sure, the material that we get from caves in Europe must go back to about 100,000 years ago; the time of the classic Neanderthal group followed soon afterwards. We don't know why there is no earlier material in the caves; apparently they were not used before the last interglacial phase (the period just before the last great glaciation). We know that men of the classic Neanderthal group were living in caves from about 75,000 to 45,000 years ago. New radioactive carbon dates even suggest that some of the traces of culture we'll describe in this chapter may have lasted to about 35,000 years ago. Probably some of the pre-neanderthaloid types of men had also lived in caves. But we have so far found their bones in caves only in Palestine and at Fontéchevade.

THE CAVE LAYERS

In parts of France, some peasants still live in caves. In prehistoric time, many generations of people lived in them. As a result, many caves have deep layers of debris. The first people moved in and lived on the rock floor. They threw on the floor whatever they didn't want, and they tracked in mud; nobody bothered to clean house in those days. Their debris—junk and mud and garbage and what not—became packed into a layer. As time went on, and generations passed, the layer grew thicker. Then there might have been a break in the occupation of the cave for a while. Perhaps the game animals got scarce and the people moved away; or maybe the cave became flooded. Later on, other people moved in and

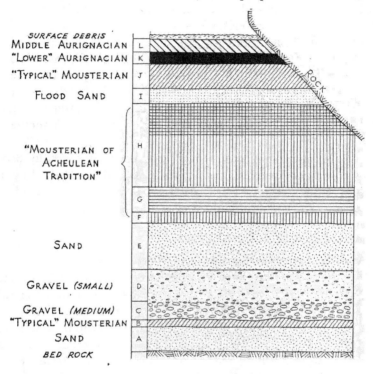

SURFACE DEBRIS		
MIDDLE AURIGNACIAN	L	
"LOWER" AURIGNACIAN	K	
"TYPICAL" MOUSTERIAN	J	
FLOOD SAND	I	
"MOUSTERIAN OF ACHEULEAN TRADITION"	H	
	G	
	F	
SAND	E	
GRAVEL (SMALL)	D	
GRAVEL (MEDIUM)	C	
"TYPICAL" MOUSTERIAN	B	
SAND	A	
BED ROCK		

SECTION OF SHELTER ON LOWER TERRACE, LE MOUSTIER

began making a new layer of their own on top of the first layer. Perhaps this process of layering went on in the same cave for a hundred thousand years; you can see what happened. The drawing on this page shows a section through such a cave. The earliest layer is on the bottom, the latest one on top. They go in order from bottom to top, earliest to latest. This is the *stratification* we talked about (p. 12).

While we may find a mix-up in caves, it's not nearly as bad as the mixing up that was done by glaciers. The animal bones and shells, the fireplaces, the bones of men, and the tools the men made all belong together, if they come from one layer. That's the reason why the cave of Peking man is so important. It is also the reason why the caves in Europe and the Near East are so important. We can get an idea of which things belong together and which lot came earliest and which latest.

In most cases, prehistoric men lived only in the mouths of caves. They didn't like the dark inner chambers as places to live in. They preferred rock-shelters, at the bases of over-hanging cliffs, if there was enough overhang to give shelter. When the weather was good, they no doubt lived in the open air as well. I'll go on using the term "cave" since it's more familiar, but remember that I really mean rock-shelter, as a place in which people actually lived.

The most important European cave sites are in Spain, France, and central Europe; there are also sites in England and Italy. A few caves are known in the Near East and Africa, and no doubt more sites will be found.

AN "INDUSTRY" DEFINED

We have already seen that the earliest European cave materials are those from the cave of Fontéchevade. Movius feels certain that the lowest materials here date back well into the third interglacial stage, that which lay between the Riss (next to the last) and the Würm I (first stage of the last) alpine glaciations. This material consists of an *industry* of stone tools, apparently all made in the flake tradition. This is the first time we have used the word "industry." It is useful to call all of the different tools found together in one layer and made of *one kind of material* an industry; that is, the tools must be found together as men left them. Tools taken from the glacial gravels (or from windswept desert surfaces or river gravels or any geological deposit) are not "together" in this sense. We might say the latter have only "geological," not "arche-ological" context. Archeological context means finding things just as men left them. We can tell what tools go to-gether in an "industrial" sense only if we have archeological context. Well-preserved cave and open-air deposits provide such context.

Up to now, the only things we could have called "industries" were the worked stone industry and perhaps the worked (?) bone industry of the Peking cave. We could add some of the very clear cases of open-air sites, like Olorgesailie and probably Torralba. We couldn't use the term for the stone tools from the glacial gravels, because we do not know which tools belonged together. But when the cave materials begin to appear in Europe, we can begin to speak of industries. Most of the European caves of this time contain industries of flint tools alone.

THE EARLIEST EUROPEAN CAVE LAYERS

We've just mentioned the industry from what is said to be the oldest inhabited cave in Europe; that is, the industry from the deepest layer of the site at Fontéchevade. Apparently it doesn't amount to much. The tools are made of stone, in the flake tradition, and are very poorly worked. This industry is called *Tayacian*. Its type tool seems to be a smallish flake tool, but there are also larger flakes which seem to have been fashioned for hacking. In fact, the type tool seems to be simply a smaller edition of the Clactonian tool (pictured on p. 45).

None of the Fontéchevade tools are really good. There are scrapers, and more or less pointed tools, and tools that may have been used for hacking and chopping. Many of the tools from the earlier glacial gravels are better made than those of this first industry we see in a European cave. There is so little of this material available that we do not know which is really typical and which is not. You would probably find it hard to see much difference between this industry and a collection of tools of the type called Clactonian, taken from the glacial gravels, especially if the Clactonian tools were small-sized.

The stone industry of the bottommost layer of the Mount Carmel cave, in Palestine, where somewhat similar tools were found, has also been called Tayacian.

I shall have to bring in many unfamiliar words for the names of the industries. The industries are usually named after the places where they were first found, and since these were in most cases in France, most of the names which follow will be of French origin. However, the names have simply become handles and are in use far beyond the boundaries of France. It would be better if we had a non-place-name terminology, but archeologists have not yet been able to agree on such a terminology.

THE ACHEULEAN INDUSTRY

Both in France and in Palestine, as well as in some African cave sites, the next layers in the deep caves have an industry in both the core-biface and the flake traditions. The core-biface tools usually make up less than half of all the tools in the industry. However, the name of the biface type of tool is generally given to the whole industry. It is called the *Acheulean*, actually a late form of it, as "Acheulean" is also used for earlier core-biface tools taken from the glacial gravels. In western Europe, the name used is *Upper Acheulean* or *Micoquian*. The same terms have been borrowed to name layers E and F in the Tabun cave, on Mount Carmel in Palestine.

The Acheulean core-biface type of tool is worked on two faces so as to give a cutting edge all around. The outline of its front view may be oval, or egg-shaped, or a quite pointed pear shape. The large chip-scars of the Acheulean core-bifaces are shallow and flat. It is suspected that this resulted from the removal of the chips with a wooden club; the deep chip-scars of the earlier Abbevillian core-biface came from beating the tool against a stone anvil. These tools are really the best and also the final products of the original Pleistocene core-biface tradition. We first noticed the tradition in the early glacial gravels (p. 43); now we see its end, but also its finest examples, in the deeper cave levels.

The flake tools, which really make up the greater bulk of this industry, are simple scrapers and chips with sharp cutting edges. The habits used to prepare them must have been pretty much the same as those used for at least one of the flake industries we shall mention presently.

There is very little else in these early cave layers. We do not have a proper "industry" of bone tools. There are traces of fire, and of animal bones, and a few shells. In Palestine, there are many more bones of deer than of gazelle in these layers; the deer lives in a wetter climate than does the gazelle. In the European cave layers, the animal bones are those of beasts that live in a warm climate. They belonged in the last

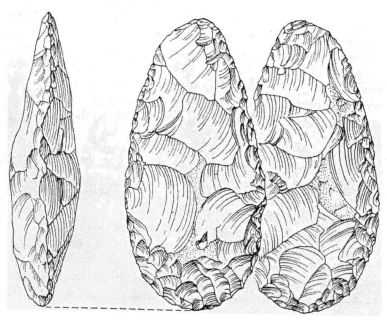

ACHEULEAN   BIFACE

interglacial period. We have not yet found the bones of fossil men definitely in place with this industry.

FLAKE INDUSTRIES FROM THE CAVES

Two more stone industries—the *Levalloisian* and the "*Mousterian*"—turn up at approximately the same time in the European cave layers. Their tools seem to be mainly in the flake tradition, but according to some of the authorities their preparation also shows some combination with the habits by which the core-biface tools were prepared.

Now notice that I don't tell you the Levalloisian and the "Mousterian" layers are both above the late Acheulean layers. Look at the cave section (p. 57) and you'll find that some

"Mousterian of Acheulean tradition" appears *above* some "typical Mousterian." This means that there may be some kinds of Acheulean industries that are later than some kinds of "Mousterian." The same is true of the Levalloisian.

There were now several different kinds of habits that men used in making stone tools. These habits were based on either one or the other of the two traditions—core-biface or flake— or on combinations of the habits used in the preparation techniques of both traditions. All were popular at about the same time. So we find that people who made one kind of stone tool industry lived in a cave for a while. Then they gave up the cave for some reason, and people with another industry moved in. Then the first people came back—or at least somebody with the same tool-making habits as the first people. Or maybe a third group of tool-makers moved in. The people who had these different habits for making their stone tools seem to have moved around a good deal. They no doubt borrowed and exchanged tricks of the trade with each other. There were no patent laws in those days.

The extremely complicated interrelationships of the different habits used by the tool-makers of this range of time are at last being systematically studied. Professor François Bordes and others have developed statistical methods of great importance for understanding these tool preparation habits.

THE LEVALLOISIAN AND MOUSTERIAN

The easiest Levalloisian tool to spot is a big flake tool. The trick in making it was to fashion carefully a big chunk of stone (called the Levalloisian "tortoise core," because it resembles the shape of a turtle-shell) and then to whack this in such a way that a large flake flew off. This large thin flake, with sharp cutting edges, is the finished Levalloisian tool. There were various other tools in a Levalloisian industry, but this is the characteristic *Levalloisian* tool.

There are several "typical Mousterian" stone tools. Different from the tools of the Levalloisian type, these were made from "disc-like cores." There are medium-sized flake "side scrapers." There are also some small pointed tools and some small "hand-axes." The last of these tool types is often a flake worked on both of the flat sides (that is, bifacially). There are also pieces of flint worked into the form of crude balls. The pointed tools may have been fixed on shafts to make short jabbing spears; the round flint balls may have been used as bolas. Actually, we don't *know* what either tool was used for. The points and side scrapers are illustrated (pp. 64 and 66).

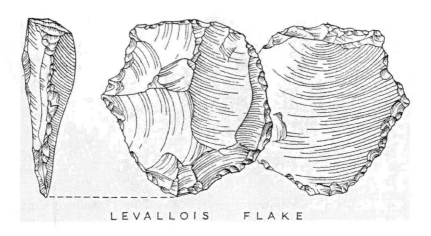

LEVALLOIS FLAKE

THE MIXING OF TRADITIONS

Nowadays the archeologists are less and less sure of the importance of any one specific tool type and name. Twenty years ago, they used to speak simply of Acheulean or Levalloisian or Mousterian tools. Now, more and more, *all* of the tools from some one layer in a cave are called an "industry," which is given a mixed name. Thus we have "Levalloiso-Mousterian," and "Acheuleo-Levalloisian," and even "Acheuleo-Mousterian" (or "Mousterian of Acheulean tradition"). Bordes' systematic work is beginning to clear up some of our confusion, and other systematic studies are beginning.

The time of these late Acheuleo-Levalloiso-Mousterioid industries is from perhaps as early as 100,000 years ago. It may have lasted until well past 50,000 years ago. This was the time of the first phase of the last great glaciation. It was also the time that the classic group of Neanderthal men was living in Europe. A number of the Neanderthal fossil finds come from these cave layers. Before the different habits of tool preparation were understood it used to be popular to say Neanderthal man was "Mousterian man." I think this is wrong. What used to be called "Mousterian" is now known to be a variety of industries with tools of both core-biface and flake habits, and so mixed that the word "Mousterian" used

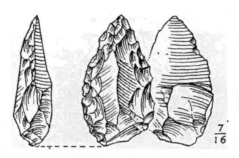

MOUSTERIAN POINT

alone really doesn't mean anything. The Neanderthalers doubtless understood each of the tool preparation habits by means of which Acheulean, Levalloisian and Mousterian type tools were produced. We also have the more modern-like Mount Carmel people, found in a cave layer of Palestine with tools almost entirely in the flake tradition, called "Levalloiso-Mousterian," and the Fontéchevade-Tayacian (p. 59).

OTHER SUGGESTIONS OF LIFE IN THE EARLY CAVE LAYERS

Except for the stone tools, what do we know of the way men lived in the time range after 100,000 to perhaps 40,000 years ago or even later? We know that in the area from Europe to Palestine, at least some of the people (some of the time) lived in the fronts of caves and warmed themselves over fires. In Europe, in the cave layers of these times, we find the bones of different animals; the bones in the lowest layers belong to animals that lived in a warm climate; above them are the bones of those who could stand the cold, like the reindeer and mammoth. Thus, the meat diet must have been changing, as the glacier crept farther south. Shells and possibly fish

Climate	Glaciers		Years B.C.	Contexts
		BEGINNING OF FOOD-PRODUCING STAGE	4,000	OPEN SITES
COLD	GL. IX-3	INDUSTRIES ADAPTED TO POST-GLACIAL ENVIRONMENT — MICROLITHS	8,000 / 10,000	
		MAGDALENIAN · SOLUTREAN · PERIGORDIAN		
COLD	GL. IX-2	VARIOUS BLADE-TOOL INDUSTRIES — EXTENDED GRAVETTIAN · MID. AURIGNACIAN · CHATELPERRONIAN	25,000	
COLD	GL. IX-1	VARIOUS BLENDED ACHEULEO-LEVALLOISO-MOUSTEROID INDUSTRIES	50,000	
		UPPER MOUSTERIAN — UPPER		
COLD	GL. III-2	ACHEULEAN — LEVALLOISIAN - TAYACIAN	100,000	
COLD	GL. III-1			
		LEVALLOISIAN	200,000	GEOLOGICAL CONTEXTS ONLY (a few embedded "workshop" sites)
COLD	GL. II-2	ACHEULEAN — CLACTONIAN		
COLD	GL. II-1	ABBEVILLIAN		
		THESE SEPARATIONS IN THE LOWER PORTION OF THE CHART EXPRESS SEPARATE TOOL-PREPARATION HABITS ONLY — THE MAKERS OF THE DIFFERENT TOOLS MAY WELL HAVE BEEN THE SAME PEOPLE!	450,000	
COLD	GL. I-2	CORE-BIFACE TOOL PREPARATION HABIT · MIXED FLAKE & CORE-BIFACE PREPARATION HABIT · FLAKE PREPARATION HABIT - WITH PLAIN OR WITH PREPARED PLATFORM · FLAKE PREPARATION HABIT - WITH PREPARED PLATFORM · FLAKE PREPARATION HABIT - WITH PLAIN PLATFORM		
COLD	GL. I-1	THE EARLY TOOL-PREPARATION TRADITIONS	600,000	

CHART SHOWING PRESENT UNDERSTANDING OF RELATIONSHIPS AND SUCCESSION OF TOOL-PREPARATION TRADITIONS, INDUSTRIES, AND ASSEMBLAGES OF WEST-CENTRAL EUROPE

Wavy lines indicate transitions in industrial habits. These transitions are not yet understood in detail. The glacial and climatic scheme shown is the alpine one. An open-air site such as Torralba is an exception to the rule of only geological context below the dotted red line.

bones have lasted in these cave layers, but there is not a trace of the vegetable foods and the nuts and berries and other wild fruits that must have been eaten when they could be found.

Bone tools have also been found from this period. Some are called scrapers, and there are also long chisel-like leg-bone

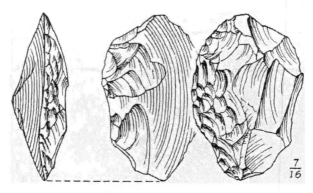

MOUSTERIAN   SIDE   SCRAPER

fragments believed to have been used for skinning animals. Larger hunks of bone, which seem to have served as anvils or chopping blocks, are fairly common.

Bits of mineral, used as coloring matter, have also been found. We don't know what the color was used for.

There is a small but certain number of cases of intentional burials. These burials have been found on the floors of the caves; in other words, the people dug graves in the places where they lived. The holes made for the graves were small. For this reason (or perhaps for some other?) the bodies were in a curled-up or contracted position. Flint or bone tools or pieces of meat seem to have been put in with some of the bodies. In several cases, flat stones had been laid over the graves.

TOOLS FROM AFRICA AND ASIA ABOUT
    100,000 YEARS AGO

Professor Movius characterizes early prehistoric Africa as a continent showing a variety of stone industries. Some of industries were purely local developments and some were ethetically identical with industries found in Europe at the same time. From northwest Africa to Capetown—excepting he tropical rain forest region of the west center—tools of eveloped Acheulean, Levalloisian, and Mousterian types have been recognized. Often they carry African place names.

In east and south Africa lived people whose industries show a development of the Levalloisian technique. Such industries are called Stillbay. Another industry, developed on the basis of the Acheulean technique, is called Fauresmith. From the northwest comes an industry with tanged points and flake-blades; this is called the Aterian. The tropical rain forest region contained people whose stone tools apparently show adjustment to this peculiar environment. Professor Desmond Clark considers this to have been the case with the so-called Sangoan industry of stone picks, adzes, core-bifaces of specialized Acheulean type, and bifacial points which were probably spearheads.

In western Asia, even as far as the east coast of India, the tools of the Eurafrican core-biface and flake tool traditions continued to be used. But in the Far East, as we noted in the last chapter, men had developed characteristic stone chopper and chopping tools. This tool preparation tradition—basically a pebble tool tradition—lasted to the very end of the Ice Age.

When more intact open air sites such as that of an earlier time at Olorgesailie, and more stratified cave sites are found and excavated in Asia and Africa, we shall be able to get a more complete picture. Recently, Professor Clark's important new site, in the swampy area above Kalambo Falls in Northern Rhodesia, has yielded water-logged wooden artifacts along with an Acheulean industry. So far, however, our picture of the general cultural level of the Old World at about 100,00 years ago—and soon afterwards—is best from Europe, but is still far from complete there, too.

CULTURE AT THE BEGINNING OF THE LAST GREAT GLACIAL PERIOD

The few things we have found must indicate only a v part of the total activities of the people who lived a

All of the things they made of wood and bark, of skins, of anything soft, are gone, except for those found in such rare cases as that of Kalambo. The fact that burials were made, at least in Europe and Palestine, is pretty clear proof that the people had some notion of a life after death. But what this notion really was, or what gods (if any) men believed in, we cannot know. Dr. Movius has also reminded me of the so-called bear cults—cases in which caves have been found which contain the skulls of bears in apparently purposeful arrangement. This might suggest some notion of hoarding up the spirits or the strength of bears killed in the hunt. Probably the people lived in small groups, as hunting and food-gathering seldom provide enough food for large groups of people. These groups possibly had some kind of leader or "chief." Very likely the rude beginnings of rules for community life and politics, and even law, were being made. But what these were, we do not know. We can only guess about such things, as we can only guess about many others; for example, how the idea of a family must have been growing, and how there may have been witch doctors who made beginnings in medicine or in art, in the materials they gathered for their trade.

The stone tools help us most. They have lasted, and we can find them. As they come to us, from this cave or that, and from this layer or that, the tool industries show a variety of combinations of the different basic habits or traditions of tool preparation. This seems only natural, as the groups of people must have been very small. The mixtures and blend-
ings of the habits used in making stone tools must mean that
were also mixtures and blends in many of the other ideas
liefs of these small groups. And what this probably
that there was no one *culture* of the time. It is
unlikely that there were simply three cultures,
"Levalloisian," and "Mousterian," as has been
past. Rather there must have been a great
related cultures at about the same stage of
could say, too, that here we really begin to
that remarkable ability of men to adapt
of conditions. We shall see this

adaptive ability even more clearly as time goes on and the record becomes more complete.

Over how great an area did these loosely related cultures reach in the time 75,000 to 45,000 or even as late as 35,000 years ago? We have described stone tools made in one or another of the flake and core-biface habits, for an enormous area. It covers all of Europe, all of Africa, the Near East, and parts of India. It is perfectly possible that the flake and core-biface habits lasted on after 35,000 years ago, in some places outside of Europe. In northern Africa, for example, we are certain that they did (see chart, p. 72).

On the other hand, in the Far East (China, Burma, Java) and in northern India, the tools of the old chopper-tool tradition were still being made. Out there, we must assume, there was a different set of loosely related cultures. At least, there was a different set of loosely related habits for the making of tools. But the men who made them must have looked much like the men of the West. Their tools were different, but just as useful.

As to what the men of the West looked like, I've already hinted at all we know so far (pp. 29 ff.). The Neanderthalers were present at the time. Some more modern-like men must have been about, too, since fossils of them have turned up at Mount Carmel in Palestine, and at Teshik Tash, in Transcaspian Russia. It is still too soon to know whether certain combinations of tools within industries were made only by certain physical types of men. But since tools of both the core-biface and the flake traditions, and their blends, turn up from South Africa to England to India, it is most unlikely that only one type of man used only one particular habit in the preparation of tools. What seems perfectly clear is that men in Africa and men in India were making just as good tools— for the different uses they had for tools in their respective environments—as were the men who lived in western Europe.

EARLY Moderns

From some time in the first (Göttweig) inter-stadial or pause of the last great glaciation (say some time after about 40,000 years ago), we have more accurate dates for the European-Mediterranean area and less accurate ones for the rest of the Old World. This is probably because the effects of the last glaciation have been studied in the European-Mediterranean area more than they have been elsewhere.

A NEW TRADITION APPEARS

Something new was probably beginning to happen in the European-Mediterranean area about 40,000 years ago, though all the rest of the Old World seems to have been going on as it had been. I can't be sure of this because the information we are using as a basis for dates is very inaccurate for the areas outside of Europe and the Mediterranean.

We can at least make a guess. In Egypt and north Africa, men were still using the old methods of making stone tools. This was especially true of flake tools of the Levalloisian type, save that they were growing smaller and smaller as time went on. But at the same time, a new tradition was becoming popular in westernmost Asia and in Europe. This was the blade-tool tradition.

BLADE TOOLS

A stone blade is really just a long parallel-sided flake, as the drawing shows. It has sharp cutting edges, and makes a very useful knife. The real trick is to be able to make one. It is almost impossible to make a blade out of any stone but flint or a natural volcanic glass called obsidian. And even if you have flint or obsidian, you first have to work up a special cone-shaped "blade-core," from which to whack off blades.

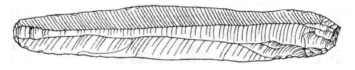

PLAIN   BLADE

You whack with a hammer stone against a bone or antler punch which is directed at the proper place on the blade-core. The blade-core has to be well supported or gripped while this is going on. To get a good flint blade tool takes a great deal of know-how.

Remember that a tradition in stone tools means no more than that some particular way of making the tools got started and lasted a long time. Men who made some tools in one tradition or set of habits would also make other tools for different purposes by means of another tradition or set of habits. It was even possible for the two sets of habits to become combined.

THE EARLIEST BLADE TOOLS

The oldest blade tools we have found were deep down in the layers of the Mount Carmel caves, in Tabun Eb and Ea. Similar tools have been found in equally early cave levels in Syria; their popularity there seems to fluctuate a bit. Some more or less parallel-sided flakes are known in the Levalloisian industry in France, but they are probably no earlier than Tabun E. The Tabun blades are part of a local late "Acheulean" industry, which is characterized by core-biface "hand axes," but which has many flake tools as well. Professor F. E.

Approximate Dates	Spain	France	Europe Otherwise	Western Asia	Egypt	Northwest Africa
8,000	"EAST SPANISH ART?"	*Chancelade*	Industries Showing Readaptation to the Post-Glacial Forest Environment — Cresswellian – Britain / Grimaldian – Italy / Vogelherd, etc. – S. Germany / Hamburgian – N. Germany / Swiderian – Moravia / Kostenki, etc. – Russia	WAD B — NATUFIAN — NATUFIAN — KEBARAN — ZARZI (Gravettian-like)	? — SEBILIAN III & SEBILIAN II	← CAPSIAN
10,000	"Cantabrian Art" MAGDALENIAN — *"Franco-"*		*Magdalenian-like In some cases*			
12,000	SOLUTREO-GRAVETTIAN — SOLUTREAN —?	IN SIX STAGES — COMBE CAPELLE – BRUNN & CRO-MAGNON / GRIMALDI	EXTENDED GRAVETTIAN — WILLENDORF	Mid-Aurignacian-like	SEBILIAN I — *Diminutive "Levalloisian"*	ATERIAN
	PARPALLO	GRAVETTIAN — HOMO SAPIENS (almost certainly present)				
16,000		↑"PERI-GORDIAN"	"CRO-MAGNON?" MIDDLE AURIGNACIAN	"Chatelperronian-like"		
25,000		COMBE CAPELLE? — CHATELPERRONIAN			KHARGAN — *"Levalloisian-like"*	
	END OF THE VARIOUS — INDUSTRIES			BARADOSTIAN (in Kurdistan) — EMIRAN (on coast)		
40,000	ACHEULEO – LEVALLOISO – MOUSTEROID — *Blades in Mt. Carmel "Acheulean"*					
MUCH COMPRESSED SCALE ↑	CORE-BIFACE AND FLAKE TRADITIONS PRESENT					
600,000	ABBEVILLIAN	AND CLACTONIAN AGGREGATIONS PRESENT		500,000 B.C.		
	Evidence for Geochronological Dating Exists			Positions Fixed by Tool Similarities Alone		

SUCCESSION OF ICE AGE FLINT TYPES, INDUSTRIES, AND ASSEMBLAGES, AND OF FOSSIL MEN, IN NORTHWESTERN EURAFRASIA

Zeuner believes that this industry may be more than 120,000 years old while Professor Bordes believes it to be much later; actually its date has not yet been fixed, but it must be old—older than the fossil finds of modern-like men in the same caves.

For some reason, the habit of making blades in Palestine and Syria was interrupted. Blades only reappeared there at about the same time they were first made in Europe, some time after 40,000 years ago; that is, after the first phase of the last glaciation was ended.

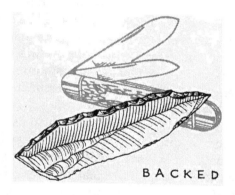

BACKED   BLADE

We are not sure just where the earliest *persisting* habits for the production of blade tools developed. Impressed by the very early momentary appearance of blades at Tabun on Mount Carmel, Professor Dorothy A. Garrod first favored the Near East as a center of origin. She spoke of "some as yet unidentified Asiatic centre," which she thought might be in the highlands of Iran or just beyond. We now know that an early blade industry in Iraqi Kurdistan, called the Baradostian by its discoverer, Professor Ralph Solecki, must date back at least about 35,000 years. At a nearby site in Iranian Kurdistan, Dr. Bruce Howe believes there may be a gradual transition from the local Mousterian into the Baradostian. But we are not on sure ground yet. When the blade tools reappear in the Syro-Palestinian area, they do so in industries which also include Levalloiso-Mousterian flake tools. From the point of view of form and workmanship, the blade tools themselves are not so fine as those which seem to be making their appearance in western Europe about the same time. There is a characteristic Syro-Palestinian flake point, possibly a projectile tip, called the Emiran, which is not known from Europe. The appearance of blade tools, together with Levalloiso-Mousterian flakes, continues even after the Emiran point has gone out of use.

It seems clear that the production of blade tools did not immediately swamp the set of older habits in Europe, too; the use of flake tools also continued there. This was not so apparent to the older archeologists, whose attention was focused on individual tool types. It is not, in fact, impossible —although it is certainly not proved—that the technique developed in the preparation of the Levalloisian tortoise core (and the striking of the Levalloisian flake from it) might have followed through to the conical core and punch technique for the production of blades. Professor Garrod is much impressed with the speed of change during the later phases of the last glaciation, and its probable consequences. She speaks of "the greater number of industries having enough individual character to be classified as distinct . . . since evolution now starts to outstrip diffusion." Her "evolution" here is of course an industrial evolution rather than a biological one. Certainly the people of Europe had begun to make blade tools during the warm spell after the first phase of the last glaciation. By about 40,000 years ago blades were well established. The bones of the blade tool makers we've found so far indicate that anatomically modern men had now certainly appeared. Unfortunately, only a few fossil men have so far been found from the very beginning of the blade tool range in Europe (or elsewhere). What I certainly shall *not* tell you is that conquering bands of fine, strong, anatomically modern men, armed with superior blade tools, came sweeping out of the East to exterminate the lowly Neanderthalers. Even if we don't know exactly what happened, I'd lay a good bet it wasn't that simple.

We do know a good deal about different blade industries in Europe. Almost all of them come from cave layers. There is a great deal of complication in what we find. The chart (p. 72) tries to simplify this complication; in fact, it doubtless simplifies it too much. But it may suggest all the complication of industries which is going on at this time. You will note that the upper portion of my much simpler chart (p. 65) covers the same material (in the section marked "Various Blade-Tool Industries"). That chart is certainly too simplified.

You will realize that all this complication comes not only from the fact that we are finding more material. It is due also to the increasing ability of men to adapt themselves to a great variety of situations. Their tools indicate this adaptiveness. We know there was a good deal of climatic change at this time. The plants and animals that men used for food were changing, too. The great variety of tools and industries we now find reflects these changes and the ability of men to keep up with the times. Now, for example, is the first time we are sure that there are tools to *make* other tools. They also show men's increasing ability to adapt themselves.

SPECIAL TYPES OF BLADE TOOLS

The most useful tools that appear at this time were made from blades.

1. The "backed" blade. This is a knife made of a flint blade, with one edge purposely blunted, probably to save the user's fingers from being cut. There are several shapes of backed blades.

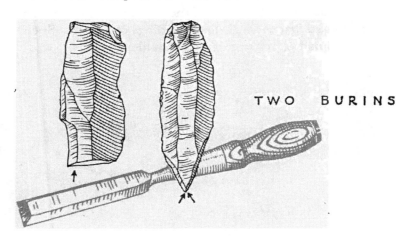

TWO BURINS

2. The *burin* or "graver." The burin was the original chisel. Its cutting edge is *transverse*, like a chisel's.

Some burins are made like a screw-driver, save that burins are sharp. Others have edges more like the blade of a chisel or a push plane, with only one bevel. Burins were probably used to make slots in wood and bone; that is, to make handles or shafts for other tools. They must also be the tools with which much of the engraving on bone (see p. 83) was done. There is a bewildering variety of different kinds of burins.

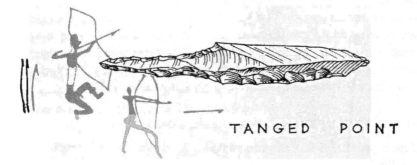

TANGED POINT

3. The "tanged" point. These stone points were used to tip arrows or light spears. They were made from blades, and they had a long tang at the bottom where they were fixed to the shaft. At the place where the tang met the main body of the stone point, there was a marked "shoulder," the beginnings of a barb. Such points had either one or two shoulders.

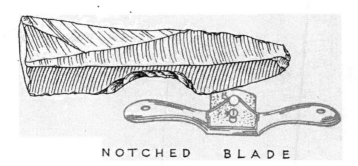

NOTCHED BLADE

4. The "notched" or "strangulated" blade. Along with the points for arrows or light spears must go a tool to

prepare the arrow or spear shaft. Today, such a tool would be called a "draw-knife" or a "spoke-shave," and this is what the notched blades probably are. Our spoke-shaves have sharp straight cutting blades and really "shave." Notched blades of flint probably scraped rather than cut.

5. The "awl," "drill," or "borer." These blade tools are worked out to a spike-like point. They must have been used for making holes in wood, bone, shell, skin, or other things.

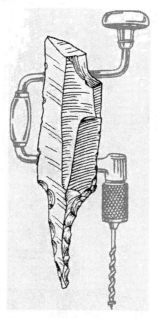

DRILL OR AWL

6. The "end-scraper on a blade" is a tool with one or both ends worked so as to give a good scraping edge. It could have been used to hollow out wood or bone, scrape hides, remove bark from trees, and a number of other things (p. 78).

There is one very special type of flint tool, which is best known from western Europe in an industry called the Solutrean. The typical Solutrean tools were not made of blades at all, although normal burins, drills, and other blade tools appear in Solutrean industries.

7. The "laurel leaf" point. Some of these tools were long and dagger-like, and must have been used as knives or daggers. Others were small, called "willow leaf,"

END-SCRAPER ON A BLADE

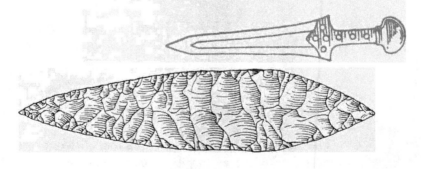

LAUREL LEAF POINT

and must have been mounted on spear or arrow shafts. Another typical Solutrean tool is the "shouldered" point. Both the "laurel leaf" and "shouldered" point types are illustrated (see above and p. 79).

The industries characterized by tools in the blade tradition also yield some flake and core tools. We will end this list with two types of tools that appear at this time. The first is made of a flake; the second is a core tool.

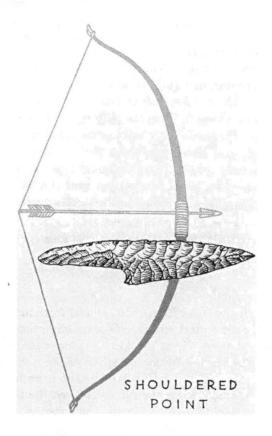

SHOULDERED
POINT

8. The "keel-shaped round scraper" is usually small and quite round, and has had chips removed up to a peak in the center. It is called "keel-shaped" because it is supposed to look (when upside down) like a section through a boat. Actually, it looks more like a tent or an umbrella. Its outer edges are sharp all the way around, and it was probably a general purpose scraping tool (see illustration, p. 81).

9. The "keel-shaped nosed scraper" is a much larger and heavier tool than the round scraper. It was made on a core with a flat bottom, and has one nicely worked end or "nose." Such tools are usually large enough to be easily grasped, and probably were used like push planes (see illustration, p. 81).

The stone tools (usually made of flint) we have just listed are among the most easily recognized blade tools, although they show differences in detail at different times. There are also many other kinds. Not all of these tools appear in any one industry at one time. Thus the different industries shown in the chart (p. 72) each have only some of the blade tools we've just listed, and also a few flake tools. Some industries even have a few core tools. The particular types of blade tools appearing in one cave layer or another, and the frequency of appearance of the different types, tell which industry we have in each layer.

OTHER KINDS OF TOOLS

By this time in Europe—say from about 40,000 to about 10,000 years ago—we begin to find other kinds of material too. Bone tools begin to appear. There are knives, pins, needles with eyes, and little double-pointed straight bars of bone that were probably fish-hooks. The fish-line would have been fastened in the center of the bar; when the fish swallowed the bait, the bar would have caught cross-wise in the fish's mouth.

One quite special kind of bone tool is a long flat point for a light spear. It has a deep notch cut up into the breadth of its base, and is called a "split-based bone point" (p. 82). We know examples of bone beads from these times, and of bone handles for flint tools. Pierced teeth of some animals were worn as beads or pendants, but I am not sure that elks' teeth were worn this early. There are even spool-shaped "buttons" or toggles.

Antler came into use for tools, especially in central and western Europe. We do not know the use of one particular antler tool that has a large hole bored in one end. One suggestion is that it was a thong-stropper used to strop or work

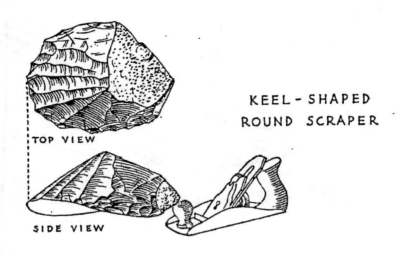

KEEL - SHAPED
ROUND SCRAPER

TOP VIEW

SIDE VIEW

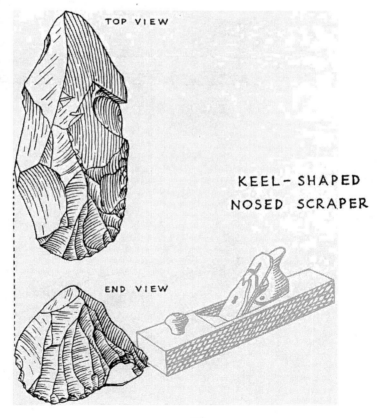

TOP VIEW

KEEL - SHAPED
NOSED SCRAPER

END VIEW

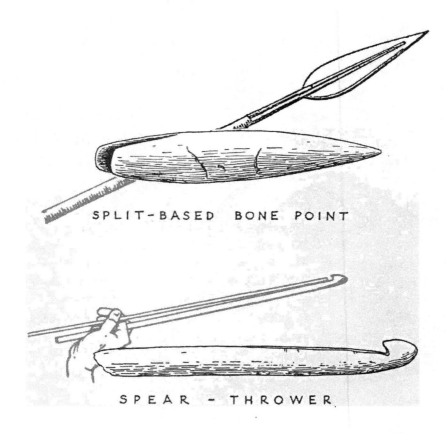

SPLIT-BASED BONE POINT

SPEAR - THROWER

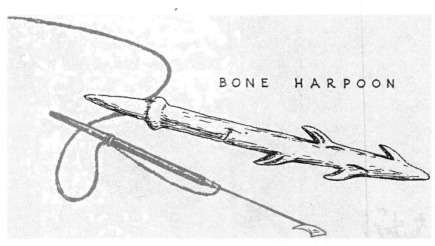

BONE HARPOON

up hide thongs (see illustration, below); another suggestion is that it was an arrow-shaft straightener.

Another interesting tool, usually of antler, is the spear-thrower, which is little more than a stick with a notch or hook on one end. The hook fits into the butt end of the spear, and the length of the spear-thrower allows you to put much more power into the throw (p. 82). It works on pretty much the same principle as the sling.

Very fancy harpoons of antler were also made in the latter half of the period in western Europe. These harpoons had barbs on one or both sides and a base which would slip out of the shaft (p. 82). Some have engraved decoration.

THE BEGINNING OF ART

In western Europe, at least, the period saw the beginning of several kinds of art work. It is handy to break the art down

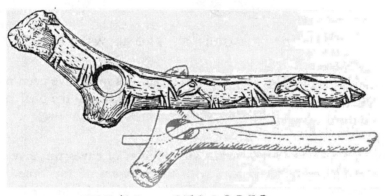

THONG - STROPPER

into two great groups: the movable art, and the cave paintings and sculpture. The movable art group includes the scratchings, engravings, and modeling which decorate tools and weapons. Knives, stroppers, spear-throwers, harpoons, and sometimes just plain fragments of bone or antler are often carved. There is also a group of large flat pebbles which seem almost to have served as sketch blocks. The surfaces of these various objects may show animals, or rather abstract floral designs, or geometric designs.

Some of the movable art is not done on tools. The most remarkable examples of this class are little figures of women. These women seem to be pregnant, and their most female characteristics are much emphasized. It is thought that these

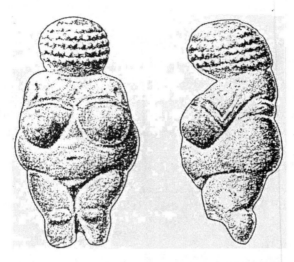

"VENUS" FIGURINE FROM WILLENDORF

"Venus" or "Mother-goddess" figurines may have been meant to show the great forces of nature—fertility and the birth of life.

CAVE PAINTINGS

In the paintings on walls and ceilings of caves we have some examples that compare with the best art of any time. The subjects were usually animals, the great cold-weather beasts of the end of the Ice Age: the mammoth, the woolly rhinoceros, the bison, the reindeer, the wild horse, the bear, the wild boar, and wild cattle. As in the movable art, there are different styles in the cave art. The really great cave art is pretty well restricted to southern France and Cantabrian (northwestern) Spain.

There are several interesting things about the "Franco-Cantabrian" cave art. It was done deep down in the darkest and most dangerous parts of the caves, although the men lived only in the openings of caves. If you think what they must have had for lights—crude lamps of hollowed stone have been found, which must have burned some kind of oil or grease, with a matted hair or fiber wick—and of the animals that may have lurked in the caves, you'll understand the part about danger. Then, too, we're sure the pictures these people painted were not simply to be looked at and admired, for they painted one picture right over other pictures which had been done earlier. Clearly, it was the *act* of *painting* that counted. The painter had to go way down into the most mysterious depths of the earth and create an animal in paint. Possibly he believed that by doing this he gained some sort of magic power over the same kind of animal when he hunted it in the open air. It certainly doesn't look as if he cared very much about the picture he painted—as a finished product to be admired—for he or somebody else soon went down and painted another animal right over the one he had done.

The cave art of the Franco-Cantabrian style is one of the great artistic achievements of all time. The subjects drawn are almost always the larger animals of the time: the bison, wild ·cattle and horses, the woolly rhinoceros, the mammoth, the wild boar, and the bear. In some of the best examples, the beasts are drawn in full color and the paintings are remarkably alive and charged with energy. They come from the hands of men who knew the great animals well—knew the feel of their fur, the tremendous drive of their muscles, and the danger one faced when he hunted them.

Other artistic styles have been found in eastern Spain and in Africa and the eastern Mediterranean. They sometimes include lively drawings, often of people hunting with bow and arrow. The East Spanish art is found on open rock faces and in rock-shelters. It is less spectacular and apparently more recent than the Franco-Cantabrian cave art.

LIFE AT THE END OF THE ICE AGE
IN EUROPE

Life in these times was probably as good as a hunter could expect it to be. Game and fish seem to have been plentiful;

berries and wild fruits probably were, too. From France to Russia, great pits or piles of animal bones have been found. Some of this killing was done as our Plains Indians killed the buffalo—by stampeding them over steep river banks or cliffs. There were also good tools for hunting, however. In western Europe, people lived in the openings of caves and under overhanging rocks. On the great plains of eastern Europe, very crude huts were being built, half underground. The first part of this time must have been cold, for it was the middle and end phases of the last great glaciation. Northern Europe from Scotland to Scandinavia, northern Germany and Russia, and also the higher mountains to the south, were certainly covered with ice. But people had fire, and the needles and tools used for scraping hides must mean that they wore clothing.

It is clear that men were thinking of a great variety of things beside the tools that helped them get food and shelter. Such burials as we find have more grave-gifts than before. Beads and ornaments and often flint, bone, or antler tools are included in the grave, and sometimes the body is sprinkled with red ochre. Red is the color of blood, which means life, and of fire, which means heat. Professor Childe wonders if the red ochre was a pathetic attempt at magic—to give back to the body the heat that had gone from it. But pathetic or not, it is sure proof that these people were already moved by death as men still are moved by it.

Their art is another example of the direction the human mind was taking. And when I say human, I mean it in the fullest sense, for this is the time in which fully modern man has appeared. On page 34, we spoke of the Cro-Magnon group and of the Combe Capelle-Brünn group of Caucasoids and of the Grimaldi "Negroids," who are no longer believed to be Negroid. I doubt that any one of these groups produced most of the achievements of the times. It's not yet absolutely sure which particular group produced the great cave art. The artists were almost certainly a blend of several (no doubt already mixed) groups. The pair of Grimaldians were buried in a grave with a sprinkling of red ochre, and were provided with shell beads and ornaments and with some blade tools of flint. Regardless of the different names once given them by the human paleontologists, each of these groups seems to have shared equally in the cultural achievements of the times, for all that the archeologists can say.

MICROLITHS

One peculiar set of tools seems to serve as a marker for the very last phase of the Ice Age in southwestern Europe. This tool-

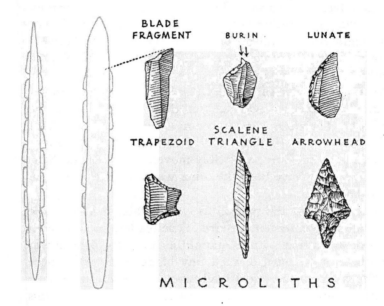

making habit is also found about the shore of the Mediterranean basin, and it moved into northern Europe as the last glaciation pulled northward. People began making blade tools of very small size. They learned how to chip very slender and tiny blades from a prepared core. Then they made these little blades into tiny triangles, half-moons ("lunates"), trapezoids, and several other geometric forms. These little tools are called "microliths." They are so small that most of them must have been fixed in handles or shafts.

We have found several examples of microliths mounted in shafts. In northern Europe, where their use soon spread, the microlithic triangles or lunates were set in rows down each side of a bone or wood point. One corner of each little triangle stuck out, and the whole thing made a fine barbed harpoon. In historic times in Egypt, geometric trapezoidal microliths were still in use as arrowheads. They were fastened—broad end out—on the end of an arrow shaft. It seems queer to give an arrow a point shaped like a "T." Actually, the little points were very sharp, and must have pierced the hides of animals very easily. We also think that the broader cutting edge of the point may have caused more bleeding than a pointed arrowhead would. In hunting fleet-footed animals like the gazelle, which might run for miles after being shot with an arrow, it was an advantage to cause as much bleeding as possible, for the animal would drop sooner.

We are not really sure where the microliths were first invented. There is some evidence that they appear early in the Near East. Their use was very common in northwest Africa but this came later. The microlith makers who reached south Russia and central Europe possibly moved up out of the Near East. Or it may have been the other way around; we simply don't yet know.

Remember that the microliths we are talking about here were made from carefully prepared little blades, and are often geometric in outline. Each microlithic industry proper was made up, in good part, of such tiny blade tools. But there were also some normal-sized blade tools and even some flake scrapers, in most microlithic industries. I emphasize this bladelet and the geometric character of the microlithic industries of the western Old World, since there has sometimes been confusion in the matter. Sometimes small flake chips, utilized as minute pointed tools, have been called "microliths." They may be *microlithic* in size in terms of the general meaning of the word, but they do not seem to belong to the sub-tradition of the blade tool preparation habits which we have been discussing here.

LATER BLADE-TOOL INDUSTRIES OF THE NEAR EAST AND AFRICA

The blade-tool industries of normal size we talked about earlier spread from Europe to central Siberia. We noted that blade tools were made in western Asia too, and early, although Professor Garrod is no longer sure that the whole tradition originated in the Near East. If you look again at my chart (p. 72) you will note that in western Asia I list some of the names of the western European industries, but with the qualification "-like" (for example, "Gravettian-like"). The western Asiatic blade-tool industries do vaguely recall some aspects of those of western Europe, but we would probably be better off if we used completely local names for them. The "Emiran" of my chart is such an example; its industry includes a long spike-like blade point which has no western European counterpart.

When we last spoke of Africa (p. 66), I told you that stone tools there were continuing in the Levalloisian flake tradition, and were becoming smaller. At some time during this process, two new tool types appeared in northern Africa: one was the Aterian point with a tang (p. 67), and the other was a sort of "laurel leaf" point, called the "Sbaikian." These two tool types were both produced from flakes. The Sbaikian points, especially, are roughly similar to some of the Solutrean points of Europe. It has been suggested that both the Sbaikian and Aterian points may be seen on their way to France through their appearance in the Spanish cave deposits of Parpallo, but there is also a rival "pre-Solutrean" in central Europe. We still do not know whether there was any contact between the makers of these north African tools and the Solutrean tool-makers. What does seem clear is that the blade-tool tradition itself arrived late in northern Africa.

NETHER AFRICA

Blade tools and "laurel leaf" points and some other probably late stone tool types also appear in central and southern Africa. There are geometric microliths on bladelets and even some coarse pottery in east Africa. There is as yet no good way of telling just where these items belong in time; in broad geological terms they are "late." Some people have guessed that they are as early as similar European and Near Eastern examples, but I doubt it. The makers of small-sized Levalloisian flake tools appear to have occupied much of Africa until very late in time. It is unfortunate that most prehistoric work in Africa has tended to concentrate on the earlier periods. We really need many more and later sites like the one at Kalambo.

THE FAR EAST

India and the Far East still seem to be going their own way. In India, some blade tools have been found. These are not well dated, save that we believe they must be post-Pleistocene. In the Far East it looks as if the old chopper-tool tradition was still continuing. For Burma, Dr. Movius feels this is fairly certain; for China he feels even more certain. Actually, we know very little about the Far East at about the time of the last glaciation. As in Africa, the major prehistoric work has tended to be concentrated on the earlier periods. In fact, far too little work has been done at all, and—even in spite of Movius's excellent example to the contrary—scholars have seemed to feel that Asia *must* have developed just as Europe did. Detailed knowledge of the later Pleistocene prehistory of Asia would have a far broader interest than for Asia alone, as you will soon see!

THE NEW WORLD BECOMES INHABITED

At some time toward the end of the last great glaciation— almost certainly after 20,000 years ago—people began to move over Bering Strait, from Asia into America. As you know, the American Indians have been assumed to be basically Mongoloids. New studies of blood group types make this somewhat uncertain, but there is no doubt that the ancestors of the American Indians came from Asia.

The stone-tool traditions of Europe, Africa, the Near and Middle East, and central Siberia, did *not* move into the New World. With only a very few special or late exceptions, there are *no* core-bifaces, flakes, or blade tools of western Old World types in the Americas. Such things just haven't been found here.

This is why it's a shame we don't know more of the end of the chopper-tool tradition in the Far East. According to Weidenreich, the Mongoloids were in the Far East long before the end of the last glaciation. If the genetics of the blood group types do demand a non-Mongoloid ancestry for the American Indians, who else may have been in the Far East 25,000 years ago? We know a little about the habits for making stone tools which these first people brought with them, and these habits don't conform with those of the western Old World. We'd better keep our eyes open for whatever happened to the end of the chopper-tool tradition in northern China; already there are hints that it lasted late there. Also we should watch future excavations in eastern Siberia. Perhaps we shall find the chopper-tool tradition spreading up that far.

THE NEW ERA

Perhaps it comes in part from the way I read the evidence and perhaps in part it is only intuition, but I feel that the materials of this chapter suggest a new era in the ways of life. Before about 40,000 years ago, people simply "gathered" their food, wandering over large areas to scavenge or to hunt in a simple sort of way. But here we have seen them "settling-in" more, perhaps restricting themselves in their wanderings and adapting themselves to a given locality in more intensive ways. This intensification might be suggested by the word "collecting." The ways of life we described in the earlier chapters were "food-gathering" ways, but now an era of "food-collecting" has begun. We shall see further intensifications of it in the next chapter.

End and PRELUDE

Up to the end of the last glaciation, we prehistorians have a relatively comfortable time schedule. The farther back we go the less exact we can be about time and details. Elbow-room of five, ten, even fifty or more thousands of years becomes available for us to maneuver in as we work backward in time. But now our story has come forward to the point where more exact methods of dating are at hand. The radioactive carbon method reaches back into the span of the last glaciation. There are other methods, developed by the geologists and paleobotanists, which supplement and extend the usefulness of the radioactive carbon determinations. And, happily, as our means of being more exact increases, our story grows more exciting. There are also more details of culture for us to deal with, which add to the interest.

CHANGES AT THE END OF THE ICE AGE

The last great glaciation of the Ice Age was a two-part affair, with sub-phases after the end of the second major part. In Europe the second major part of this glaciation ended somewhere around 14,000 years ago. By that time the glaciers had begun to melt back, for the last time. Remember that Professor Antevs (p. 19) isn't sure the Ice Age is over yet! This melting sometimes went by fits and starts, and the weather wasn't always changing for the better; but there was at least one time when European weather was even better than it is now.

The melting back of the glaciers and the weather fluctuations caused other changes, too. We know a fair amount about these changes in Europe. In an earlier chapter, we said that the whole Ice Age was a matter of continual change over long periods of time. As the last glaciers began to melt back some interesting things happened to mankind.

In Europe, along with the melting of the last glaciers, geography itself was changing. Britain and Ireland had certainly become islands by 5000 B.C. The Baltic was sometimes a salt sea, sometimes a large fresh-water lake. Forests began to grow where the glaciers had been, and in what had once been the cold tundra areas in front of the glaciers. The great cold-weather animals—the mammoth and the woolly rhinoceros—retreated northward and finally died out. It is probable that the efficient hunting of the earlier people of 20,000 or 25,000 to about 12,000 years ago had helped this process along (see p. 86). Europeans, especially those of the post-glacial period, had to keep changing to keep up with the times.

The archeological materials for the time from 10,000 to 6000 B.C. seem simpler than those of the previous five thousand years. The great cave art of France and Spain had gone; so had the fine carving in bone and antler. Smaller, speedier animals were moving into the new forests. New ways of hunting them, or ways of getting other food, had to be found. Hence, new tools and weapons were necessary. Some of the people who moved into northern Germany were successful reindeer hunters. Then the reindeer moved off to the north, and again new sources of food had to be found.

THE READJUSTMENTS COMPLETED IN EUROPE

After a few thousand years, things began to look better. Or at least we can say this: By about 6000 B.C. we again get better archeological materials. The best of these come from the north European area: Britain, Belgium, Holland, Denmark, north Germany, southern Norway and Sweden. Much of this north European material comes from bogs and swamps where it had become water-logged and has kept very well. Thus we have much more complete *assemblages*[1] than for any time earlier.

The best known of these assemblages is the *Maglemosian*, named after a great Danish peat-swamp where much has been found.

In the Maglemosian assemblage the flint industry was still very important. Blade tools, arrow points, and burins were still made, but there were also axes for cutting the trees in the new forests. Moreover, the tiny microlithic blades, in a variety of geometric forms, are also found. Thus, a specialized tradition that possibly began east of the Mediterranean had reached northern Europe. There was also a ground stone industry; some axes and club-heads were made by grinding and polishing rather than by chipping. The industries in bone and antler show a great variety of tools: axes, fish-hooks, fish spears, handles and hafts for other tools, harpoons, and clubs.

---

[1] "Assemblage" is a useful word when there are different kinds of archeological materials belonging together, from one area and of one time. An assemblage is made up of a number of "industries" (that is, all the tools in chipped stone, all the tools in bone, all the tools in wood, the traces of houses, etc.) and everything else that manages to survive, such as the art, the burials, the bones of the animals used as food, and the traces of plant foods; in fact, everything that has been left to us and can be used to help reconstruct the lives of the people to whom it once belonged. Our own present-day "assemblage" would be the sum total of all the objects in our mail-order catalogues, department stores and supply houses of every sort, our churches, our art galleries and other buildings, together with our roads, canals, dams, irrigation ditches, and any other traces we might leave of ourselves, from graves to garbage dumps. Not everything would last, so that an archeologist digging us up—say 2,000 years from now—would find only the most durable items in our assemblage.

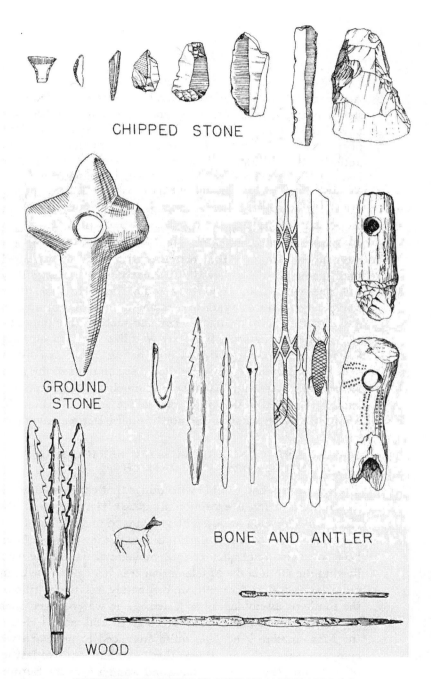

CHIPPED STONE

GROUND STONE

BONE AND ANTLER

WOOD

SKETCH OF MAGLEMOSIAN ASSEMBLAGE

A remarkable industry in wood has been preserved. Paddles, sled runners, handles for tools, and bark floats for fish-nets have been found. There are even fish-nets made of plant fibers. Canoes of some kind were no doubt made. Bone and antler tools were decorated with simple patterns, and amber was collected. Wooden bows and arrows are found.

It seems likely that the Maglemosian bog finds are remains of summer camps, and that in winter the people moved to higher and drier regions. Childe calls them the "Forest folk"; they probably lived much the same sort of life as did our pre-agricultural Indians of the north central states. They hunted small game or deer; they did a great deal of fishing; they collected what plant food they could find. In fact, their assemblage shows us again that remarkable ability of men to adapt themselves to change. They had succeeded in domesticating the dog; he was still a very wolf-like dog, but his long association with mankind had now begun. Professor Coon believes that these people were direct descendants of the men of the glacial age and that they had much the same appearance. He believes that most of the Ice Age survivors still extant are living today in the northwestern European area.

SOUTH AND CENTRAL EUROPE PERHAPS AS READJUSTED AS THE NORTH

There is always one trouble with things that come from areas where preservation is exceptionally good: The very quantity of materials in such an assemblage tends to make things from other areas look poor and simple, although they may not have been so originally at all. The assemblages of the people who lived to the south of the Maglemosian area may also have been quite large and varied; but, unfortunately, relatively little of the southern assemblages has lasted. The water-logged sites of the Maglemosian area preserved a great deal more. Hence the Maglemosian itself *looks* quite advanced to us, when we compare it with the few things that have happened to last in other areas. If we could go back and wander over the Europe of eight thousand years ago, we would probably find that the peoples of France, central Europe, and south central Russia were just as advanced as those of the north European-Baltic belt.

South of the north European belt the hunting–food-collecting peoples were living on as best they could during this time. One interesting group, which seems to have kept to the regions of sandy soil and scrub forest, made great quantities of geometric microliths. These are the materials called *Tardenoisian*. The materials of the "Forest folk" of France and central Europe generally are called *Azilian;* Dr. Movius believes the term might best be restricted to the area south of the Loire River.

HOW MUCH REAL CHANGE WAS THERE?

You can see that no really *basic* change in the way of life has yet been described. Childe sees the problem that faced the Europeans of 10,000 to 4000 B.C. as a problem in readaptation to the post-glacial forest environment. By 6000 B.C. some quite successful solutions of the problem—like the Maglemosian—had been made. The upsets that came with the melting of the last ice gradually brought about all sorts of changes in the tools and food-getting habits, but the people themselves were still just as much simple hunters, fishers, and food collectors as they had been in 25,000 B.C. It could be said that they changed just enough so that they would not have to change. But there is a bit more to it than this.

Professor Mathiassen of Copenhagen, who knows the archeological remains of this time very well, poses a question. He speaks of the material as being neither rich nor progressive, in fact "rather stagnant," but he goes on to add that the people had a certain "receptiveness" and were able to adapt themselves quickly when the next change did come. My own understanding of the situation is that the "Forest folk" made nothing as spectacular as had the producers of the earlier Magdalenian assemblage and the Franco-Cantabrian art. On the other hand, they *seem* to have been making many more different kinds of tools for many more different kinds of tasks than had their Ice Age forerunners. I emphasize "seem" because the preservation in the Maglemosian bogs is very complete; certainly we cannot list anywhere near as many different things for earlier times as we did for the Maglemosians (p. 94). I believe this experimentation with all kinds of new tools and gadgets, this intensification of adaptiveness (p. 91), this "receptiveness," even if it is still only pointed toward hunting, fishing, and food-collecting, is an important thing.

Remember that the only marker we have handy for the *beginning* of this tendency toward "receptiveness" and experimentation is the little microlithic blade tools of various geometric forms. These, we saw, began before the last ice had melted away, and they lasted on in use for a very long time. I wish there were a better marker than the microliths but I do not know of one. Remember, too, that as yet we can only use the microliths as a marker in Europe and about the Mediterranean.

CHANGES IN OTHER AREAS?

All this last section was about Europe. How about the rest of the world when the last glaciers were melting away?

We simply don't know much about this particular time in other parts of the world except in Europe, the Mediterranean basin and the Middle East. People were certainly continuing to move into the New World by way of Siberia and the Bering Strait about this time. But for the greater part of Africa and Asia, we do not know exactly what was happening. Some day, we shall no doubt find out; today we are without very much clear information.

REAL CHANGE AND PRELUDE IN THE NEAR EAST

The appearance of the microliths and the developments made by the "Forest folk" of northwestern Europe also mark an end. They show us the terminal phase of the old food-collecting way of life. It grows increasingly clear that at about the same time that the Maglemosian and other "Forest folk" were adapting themselves to hunting, fishing, and collecting in new ways to fit the post-glacial environment, something completely new was being made ready in southwestern Asia.

Unfortunately, we do not have as much understanding of the climate and environment of the late Ice Age in southwestern Asia as we have for most of Europe. Probably the weather was never so violent or life quite so rugged as it was in northern Europe. We know that the microliths made their appearance in western Asia at least by 10,000 B.C. and probably earlier, marking the beginning of the terminal phase of food-collecting. Then, gradually, we begin to see the build-up towards the first *basic change* in human life.

This change amounted to a revolution just as important as the Industrial Revolution. In it, men first learned to domesticate plants and animals. They began *producing* their food instead of simply gathering or collecting it. When their food-production became reasonably effective, people could and did settle down in village-farming communities. With the appearance of the little farming villages, a new way of life was actually under way. Professor Childe has good reason to speak of the "food-producing revolution," for it was indeed a revolution.

QUESTIONS ABOUT CAUSE

We do not yet know *how* and *why* this great revolution took place. We are only just beginning to put the questions properly. I suspect the answers will concern some delicate and subtle interplay between man and nature. Clearly, both the level of culture and the natural condition of the environment must have been ready for the great change, before the change itself could come about.

It is going to take years of co-operative field work by both archeologists and the natural scientists who are most helpful to them before the *how* and *why* answers begin to appear. Anthropologically trained archeologists are fascinated with the cultures of men in times of great change. About ten or twelve thousand years ago, the general level of culture in many parts of the world seems to have been ready for change. In northwestern Europe, we saw that cultures "changed just enough so that they would not have to change." We linked this to environmental changes with the coming of post-glacial times.

In southwestern Asia, we archeologists can prove that the food-producing revolution actually took place. We can see *the* important consequence of effective domestication of plants and animals in the appearance of the settled village-farming community. And within the village-farming community was the seed of civilization. The way in which effective domestication of plants and animals came about, however, must also be linked closely with the natural environment. Thus the archeologists will not solve the *how* and *why* questions alone—they will need the help of interested natural scientists in the field itself.

PRECONDITIONS FOR THE REVOLUTION

Especially at this point in our story, we must remember how culture and environment go hand in hand. Neither plants nor animals domesticate themselves; men domesticate them. Furthermore, men usually domesticate only those plants and animals which are useful. There is a good question here: What is cultural usefulness? But I shall side-step it to save time. Men cannot domesticate plants and animals that do not exist in the environment where the men live. Also, there are certainly some animals and probably some plants that resist domestication, although they might be useful.

This brings me back again to the point that *both* the level of culture and the natural condition of the environment—with the proper plants and animals in it—must have been ready before domestication could have happened. But this is precondition, not cause. Why did effective food-production happen first in the Near East? Why did it happen independently in the New World, and only slightly later, too? Why also in the Far East? Why did it happen at all? Why are all human beings not still living as the Maglemosians did? These are the questions we still have to face.

CULTURAL "RECEPTIVENESS" AND PROMISING ENVIRONMENTS

Until the archeologists and the natural scientists—botanists, geologists, zoologists, and general ecologists—have spent many more years on the problem, we shall not have full *how* and *why* answers. I do think, however, that we are beginning to understand what to look for.

We shall have to learn much more about what makes the cultures of men "receptive" and experimental. Did change in the environment alone force it? Was it simply a case of Professor Toynbee's "challenge and response?" I cannot believe the answer is quite that simple. Were it so simple, we should want to know why the change hadn't come earlier, along with earlier environmental changes. We shall not know the answer, however, until we have excavated the traces of many more cultures of the time in question. We shall doubtless also have to learn more about, and think imaginatively about, the simpler cultures still left today. The "mechanics" of culture in general will be bound to interest us.

It will also be necessary to learn more about the environments of 10,000 to 12,000 years ago. In which regions of the world were the natural conditions most promising? Did this promise include plants and animals which could be domesticated, or did it only offer new ways of food-collecting? There is much work to do on this problem, but we are beginning to get some general hints.

Before I begin to detail the hints we now have from western Asia, I want to do two things. First, I shall tell you of an old theory as to how food-production might have appeared. Second, I shall bother you with some definitions which should help us in our thinking as the story goes on.

AN OLD THEORY AS TO THE CAUSE OF
   THE REVOLUTION

The idea that change would result, if the balance between nature and culture became upset, is of course not a new one. For at least twenty-five years, there has been a general theory as to *how* the food-producing revolution happened. This theory depends directly on the idea of natural change in the environment.

The five thousand years following about 10,000 B.C. must have been very difficult ones, the theory begins. These were the years when the most marked melting of the last glaciers was going on. While the glaciers were in place, the climate to the south of them must have been different from the climate in those areas today. You have no doubt read that people once lived in regions now covered by the Sahara Desert. This is true; just when is not entirely clear. The theory is that during the time of the glaciers, there was a broad belt of rain winds south of the glaciers. These rain winds would have kept north Africa, the Nile Valley, and the Middle East green and fertile. But when the glaciers melted back to the north, the belt of rain winds is supposed to have moved north too. Then the people living south and east of the Mediterranean would have found that their water supply was drying up, that the animals they hunted were dying or moving away, and that the plant foods they collected were dried up and scarce.

According to the theory, all this would have been true except in the valleys of rivers and in oases in the growing deserts. Here, in the only places where water was left, the men and animals and plants would have clustered. They would have been forced to live close to one another, in order to live at all. Presently the men would have seen that some animals were more useful or made better food than others, and so they would have begun to protect these animals from their natural enemies. The men would also have been forced to try new plant foods—foods which possibly had to be prepared before they could be eaten. Thus, with trials and errors, but by being forced to live close to plants and animals, men would have learned to domesticate them.

THE OLD THEORY TOO SIMPLE FOR THE FACTS

This theory was set up before we really knew anything in detail about the later prehistory of the Near and Middle East. We now know that the facts which have been found don't fit the old theory at all well. Also, I have yet to find an American meteorologist who feels that we know enough about the changes in the weather pattern to say that it can have been so simple and direct. And, of course, the glacial ice which began melting after 12,000 years ago was merely the last sub-phase of the last great glaciation. There had also been three earlier periods of great alpine glaciers, and long periods of warm weather in between. If the rain belt moved north as the glaciers melted for the last time, it must have moved in the same direction in earlier times. Thus, the forced neighborliness of men, plants, and animals in river valleys and oases must also have happened earlier. Why didn't domestication happen earlier, then?

Furthermore, it does not seem to be in the oases and river valleys that we have our first or only traces of either food-production or the earliest farming villages. These traces are also in the hill-flanks of the mountains of western Asia. Our earliest sites of the village-farmers do not seem to indicate a greatly different climate from that which the same region now shows. In fact, everything we now know suggests that the old theory was just too simple an explanation to have been the true one. The only reason I mention it—beyond correcting the ideas you may get in the general texts—is that it illustrates the kind of thinking we shall have to do, even if it is doubtless wrong in detail.

We archeologists shall have to depend much more than we ever have on the natural scientists who can really help us. I can tell you this from experience. I had the great good fortune to have on my expedition staff in Iraq in 1954–55, and in Iran in 1959–60, a geologist, a botanist, and a zoologist. Their studies added whole new bands of color to my spectrum of thinking about *how* and *why* the revolution took place and how the village-farming community began. But this is only a beginning; as I said earlier, we are just now learning to ask the proper questions.

ABOUT STAGES AND ERAS

Now come some definitions, so I may describe my material more easily. Archeologists have always loved to make divisions and subdivisions within the long range of materials which they have found. They often disagree violently about which particular assemblage of material goes into which subdivision, about what the subdivisions should be named, about what the subdivisions really mean culturally. Some archeologists, probably through habit, favor an old scheme of Grecized names for the subdivisions: paleolithic, mesolithic, neolithic. I refuse to use these words myself. They have meant too many different things to too many different people and have tended to hide some pretty fuzzy thinking. Probably you haven't even noticed my own scheme of subdivision up to now, but I'd better tell you in general what it is.

I think of the earliest great group of archeological materials, from which we can deduce only a food-gathering way of culture, as the *food-gathering stage*. I say "stage" rather than "age," because it is not quite over yet; there are still a few primitive people in out-of-the-way parts of the world who remain in the food-gathering stage. In fact, Professor Julian Steward would probably prefer to call it a food-gathering *level* of existence, rather than a stage. This would be perfectly acceptable to me. I also tend to find myself using *collecting*, rather than *gathering*, for the more recent aspects or era of the stage, as the word "collecting" appears to have more sense of purposefulness and specialization than does "gathering" (see p. 91).

Now, while I think we could make several possible subdivisions of the food-gathering stage—I call my subdivisions of stages *eras*[1]—I believe the only one which means much to us here is the last or *terminal sub-era of food-collecting* of the whole food-gathering stage. The microliths seem to mark its approach in the northwestern part of the Old World. It is really shown best in the Old World by the materials of the "Forest folk," the cultural adaptation to the post-glacial environment in northwestern Europe. We talked about the

---

[1] It is difficult to find words which have a sequence or gradation of meaning with respect to both development and a range of time in the past, or with a range of time from somewhere in the past which is perhaps not yet ended. One standard Webster definition of *stage* is: "One of the steps into which the material development of man .... is divided." I cannot find any dictionary definition that suggests which of the words, *stage* or *era*, has the meaning of a longer span of time. Therefore, I have chosen to let my eras be shorter, and to subdivide my stages into eras. Webster gives *era* as: "A signal stage of history, an epoch." When I want to subdivide my eras, I find myself using *sub-eras*. Thus I speak of the *eras* within a *stage* and of the *sub-eras* within an *era*; that is, I do so when I feel that I really have to, and when the evidence is clear enough to allow it.

"Forest folk" at the beginning of this chapter, and I used the Maglemosian assemblage of Denmark as an example.

The food-producing revolution ushers in the *food-producing stage*. This stage began to be replaced by the *industrial stage* only about two hundred years ago. Now notice that my stage divisions are in terms of technology and economics. We must think sharply to be sure that the subdivisions of the stages, the eras, are in the same terms. This does not mean that I think technology and economics are the only important realms of culture. It is rather that for most of prehistoric time the materials left to the archeologists tend to limit our deductions to technology and economics.

I'm so soon out of my competence, as conventional ancient history begins, that I shall only suggest the earlier eras of the food-producing stage to you. This book is about prehistory, and I'm not a universal historian.

THE TWO EARLIEST ERAS OF THE FOOD-PRODUCING STAGE

The food-producing stage seems to appear in western Asia with really revolutionary suddenness. It is seen by the relative speed with which the traces of new crafts appear in the earliest village-farming community sites we've dug. It is seen by the spread and multiplication of these sites themselves, and the remarkable growth in human population we deduce from this increase in sites. We'll look at some of these sites and the archeological traces they yield in the next chapter. When such village sites begin to appear, I believe we are in the *era of the primary village-farming community*. I also believe this is the second era of the food-producing stage.

The first era of the food-producing stage, I believe, was an *era of incipient cultivation and animal domestication*. I keep saying "I believe" because the actual evidence for this earlier era is so slight that one has to set it up mainly by playing a hunch for it. The reason for playing the hunch goes about as follows.

One thing we seem to be able to see, in the food-collecting era in general, is a tendency for people to begin to settle down. This settling down seemed to become further intensified in the terminal era. How this is connected with Professor Mathiassen's "receptiveness" and the tendency to be experimental, we do not exactly know. The evidence from the New World comes into play here as well as that from the Old World. With this settling down in one place, the people of the terminal era—especially the "Forest folk" whom we know best—began making a great variety of new things. I remarked about this earlier in the chapter. Dr. Robert M. Adams is of the opinion that this atmosphere of experimentation with new tools—with new ways of collecting food—is the kind of atmosphere in which one might expect trials at planting and at animal domestication to have been made. We first begin to find traces of more permanent life in outdoor camp sites, although caves were still inhabited at the beginning of the terminal era. It is not surprising at all that the "Forest folk" had already domesticated the dog. In this sense, the whole era of food-collecting was becoming ready and almost "incipient" for cultivation and animal domestication.

Northwestern Europe was not the place for really effective beginnings in agriculture and animal domestication. These would have had to take place in one of those natural environments of promise, where a variety of plants and animals, each capable of domestication, was available in the wild state. Let me spell this out. Really effective food-production must include a variety of items to make up a reasonably well-rounded diet. The food-supply so produced must be trustworthy, even though the food-producing peoples themselves might be happy to supplement it with fish and wild strawberries, just as we do when such things are available. So, as we said earlier, part of our problem is that of finding a region with a natural environment which includes—and did include, some ten thousand years ago—a variety of possibly domesticable wild plants and animals.

NUCLEAR AREAS

Now comes the last of my definitions. A region with a natural environment which included a variety of wild plants and animals, both possible and ready for domestication, would be a central or core or *nuclear area;* that is, it would be when and *if* food-production took place within it. It is pretty hard for me to imagine food-production having ever made an independent start outside such a nuclear area, although there may be some possible nuclear areas in which food-production never took place (parts of Africa, for example).

We know of several such nuclear areas. In the New World, Middle America and the Andean highlands make up one or two; it is my understanding that the evidence is not yet clear as to which. There was probably a nuclear area somewhere in southeastern Asia, in the Malay peninsula or Burma perhaps, connected with the early cultivation of taro, breadfruit, the banana and the mango. Possibly the cultivation of rice and the domestication of the chicken and of zebu cattle and the water buffalo belong to this southeast Asiatic nuclear area. We know relatively little about it archeologically, as yet. The nuclear area which was the scene of the earliest experiment in effective food-production was in southwestern Asia. Since I know it best, I shall use it as my example.

THE NUCLEAR NEAR EAST

The nuclear area of western Asia is naturally the one of greatest interest to people of the western cultural tradition. Our cultural heritage began within it. The area itself is the region of the hilly flanks of rain-watered grass-land which build up to the high mountain ridges of Iran, Iraq, Turkey, Syria, and Palestine. The map on page 125 indicates the region. If you have a good atlas, try to locate the zone which surrounds the drainage basin of the Tigris and Euphrates Rivers at elevations of from approximately 2,000 to 5,000 feet. The lower alluvial land of the Tigris-Euphrates basin itself has very little rainfall. Some years ago Professor James Henry Breasted called the alluvial lands of the Tigris-Euphrates a part of the "fertile crescent." These alluvial lands are very fertile if irrigated. Breasted was most interested in the oriental civilizations of conventional ancient history, and irrigation had become effective as they developed.

The country of grassy hills and intermontane valleys above Breasted's crescent receives from 10 to 20 or more inches of

winter rainfall each year, which is about what Kansas has.
Above this environmental zone tower the peaks and ridges of
the Lebanon-Amanus chain bordering the coast-line from
Palestine to Turkey, the Taurus Mountains of southern Turkey, and the Zagros range of the Iraq-Iran borderland. There
are now increasingly firm hints that the nuclear area stretched
to the northwest and west of the upper Tigris-Euphrates basin
proper, across some of the less elevated and fertile plains of the
Anatolian plateau in Turkey. The rugged mountain frame for
our hilly-flanks zone and its extensions rises to some magnifi-
cent alpine scenery, with peaks of from ten to fifteen thousand
feet in elevation. There are several gaps in the Mediterranean
coastal portion of the frame, through which the winter's rain-
bearing winds from the sea may break so as to carry rain to
the foothills of the Taurus and the Zagros.

The picture I hope you will have from this description is
that of an intermediate natural zone lying between or within
two regions of extremes. The lower Tigris-Euphrates basin
land is low and far too dry and hot for agriculture based on
rainfall alone; to the south and southwest, it merges directly
into the great desert of Arabia. The mountains which lie
above this natural zone are much too high and rugged to
have encouraged farmers. But how far toward the northwest
—perhaps even to the Macedonian foothills of the Balkan
Mountains—did the upper boundary of the zone lie? We
are not yet sure.

THE NATURAL ENVIRONMENT OF THE
NUCLEAR NEAR EAST

The more we learn of this hilly-flanks zone and its extensions,
the more it seems surely to have been a nuclear area. This is
where we archeologists need, and are beginning to get, the
help of natural scientists. They are coming to the conclusion
that the natural environment of the hilly-flanks zone today
is much as it was some eight to ten thousand years ago. There
are still two kinds of wild wheat and a wild barley, and the wild
sheep, goat, and pig. We have discovered traces of each
of these at about nine thousand years ago, also traces of wild
cattle and dogs, each of which appears to be the probable

ancestor of the domesticated form. In fact, at about nine thousand years ago, the two wheats, the barley, and at least the sheep and goat, were already well on the road to domestication.

The wild wheats give us an interesting clue. They are only available together with the wild barley within the hilly-flanks zone. While the wild barley grows in a variety of elevations and beyond the zone, at least one of the wild wheats does not seem to grow below the hill country. As things look at the moment, the domestication of both the wheats together could *only* have taken place within this natural zone. Barley seems to have first come into cultivation due to its presence as a weed in already cultivated wheat fields. There is also increasing certainty that the animals which were first domesticated were most at home up in this natural habitat in their wild state.

With a single exception—that of the dog—the earliest positive evidence of domestication includes the two forms of wheat, the barley, and the goat, sheep and pig. The evidence comes from within the hilly-flanks zone. However, with the probable exception of sheep, it comes from a settled village proper, Jarmo (which I'll describe in the next chapter), and is thus from the era of the primary village-farming community. We are still without positive evidence of domesticated grain in the first era of the food-producing stage, that of incipient cultivation and animal domestication, but there is increasing evidence for domesticated sheep in this first era.

THE ERA OF INCIPIENT CULTIVATION AND ANIMAL DOMESTICATION

I said above (p. 105) that my era of incipient cultivation and animal domestication is mainly set up by playing a hunch. Although we cannot really demonstrate it—and certainly not in the Near East—it would be very strange for food-collectors not to have known a great deal about the plants and animals most useful to them. We can imagine them remembering to go back, season after season, to a particular patch of ground where seeds or acorns or berries grew particularly well. Most human beings, unless they are extremely hungry, are attracted to baby animals, and many wild pups or fawns or piglets must have been brought back alive by hunting parties.

In this last sense, man has probably always been an incipient cultivator and domesticator. But I believe that Adams is right in suggesting that this would be doubly true with the experimenters of the terminal era of food-collecting. We noticed that they also seem to have had a tendency to settle down. Now my hunch goes that *when* this experimentation and settling down took place within a potential nuclear area—where a whole constellation of plants and animals possible of domestication was available—the change was easily made. The evidence certainly seems to be building up in this direction.

INCIPIENT ERAS AND NUCLEAR AREAS

I have put this scheme into a simple chart (p. 111) with the names of a few of the sites we are going to talk about. You will see that my hunch means that there are eras of incipient cultivation *only* within nuclear areas. In a nuclear area, the terminal era of food-collecting would probably have been quite short—if, in fact, it existed at all. The era of incipience *may* have followed directly out of the more generalized era of food-collecting. I do not know for how long a time the era of incipient cultivation and domestication would have lasted, but perhaps for several thousand years. Then it passed on into the era of the primary village-farming community.

Outside a nuclear area, the terminal era of food-collecting would last for a long time; in a few out-of-the-way parts of the world, it still hangs on. It would end in any particular place through contact with and the spread of ideas of people who had passed on into one of the more developed eras. In many cases, the terminal era of food-collecting was ended by the incoming of the food-producing peoples themselves. For example, the practices of food-production were carried into Europe by the actual movement of some numbers of peoples (we don't know how many) who had reached at least the level of the primary village-farming community. The "Forest folk" learned food-production from them. There was no era of incipient cultivation and domestication proper in Europe, if my hunch is right.

The way I see it, two things were required in order that an era of incipient cultivation and domestication could begin

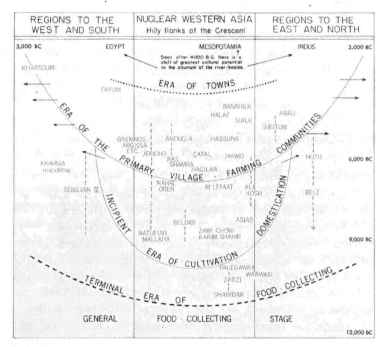

POSSIBLE RELATIONSHIPS OF STAGES AND ERAS IN
WESTERN ASIA AND NORTHEASTERN AFRICA

First, there had to be the natural environment of a nuclear area, with its whole group of plants and animals capable of domestication. This is the aspect of the matter which we've said is directly given by nature. But it is quite possible that such an environment with such a group of plants and animals in it may have existed well before ten thousand years ago in the Near East. It is also quite possible that the same promising condition may have existed in regions which never developed into nuclear areas proper. Here, again, we come back to the cultural factor. I think it was that "atmosphere of experimentation" we've talked about once or twice before.

I can't define it for you, other than to say that by the end of the Ice Age, the general level of many cultures was ready for change. Ask me how and why this was so, and I'll tell you we don't know yet; if we understood this kind of question, there would be no need for me to go on being a prehistorian!

Now since this was an era of incipience, of the birth of new ideas, and of experimentation, it is very difficult to see its traces archeologically. New tools having to do with the new ways of getting and, in fact, producing food would have taken some time to develop. It need not surprise us too much if we cannot find hoes for planting and sickles for reaping grain at the very beginning. We might expect a time of making-do with some of the older tools, or with make-shift tools, for some of the new jobs. The present-day wild cousin of the domesticated sheep still lives in the mountains of western Asia. It has no wool, only a fine down under hair like that of a deer, so it need not surprise us to find neither the whorls used for spinning nor traces of woollen cloth. It must have taken some time for a wool-bearing sheep to develop and also time for the invention of new tools for weaving. It would have been the same with other kinds of tools for the new way of life.

It is difficult even for an experienced comparative zoologist to tell which are the bones of domesticated animals and which are those of their wild cousins. This is especially so because the animal bones the archeologists find are usually fragmentary. Furthermore, we are only now gathering a sort of library collection of the skeletons of the animals and an herbarium of the plants of those areas, against which the traces which the archeologists find may be checked. In the nuclear area in the Near East, some of the wild animals, at least, have already become extinct. There are no longer any wild cattle or many wild horses in western Asia. We know they were there from the finds we've made in caves of late Ice Age times, and from some slightly later sites.

SITES WITH ANTIQUITIES OF THE INCIPIENT ERA

So far, we know only a very few sites which would suit my notion of the incipient era of cultivation and animal domestication. I am closing this chapter with descriptions of two of the best Near Eastern examples I know. You may not be satisfied that what I am able to describe makes a full-bodied era of development at all. Remember, however, that I've told you I'm largely playing a kind of a hunch, and also that the archeological materials of this era will always be extremely difficult to interpret. At the beginning of any new way of life, there will be a great tendency for people to make-do, at first, with tools and habits they are already used to. I would suspect that a great deal of this making-do went on almost to the end of this era.

THE NATUFIAN, AN ASSEMBLAGE OF THE INCIPIENT ERA

The assemblage called the Natufian comes from the upper layers of a number of caves in Palestine. Traces of its flint industry have also turned up in Syria and Lebanon. Recently, Dr. Enver Bostanci has found suggestive hints of a few Natufian-like tools at Beldibi, a cave on the south-central coast of Turkey. We don't know just how old the Natufian is. I guess that it probably falls within five hundred years either way of about 8000 B.C.

Until recently, the people who produced the Natufian assemblage were thought to have been only cave dwellers, but now at least three open air Natufian sites have been briefly described. In their best-known dwelling place, on Mount Carmel, the Natufian folk lived in the open mouth of a large rock-shelter and on the terrace in front of it. On the terrace, they had set at least two short curving lines of stones; but these were hardly architecture; they seem more like benches or perhaps the low walls of open pens. There were also one or two small clusters of stones laid like paving, and a ring of stones around a hearth or fireplace. One very round and regular basin-shaped depression had been cut into the rocky floor of the terrace, and there were other less regular basin-like depressions. In the newly reported open air sites, of which M. Jean Perrot's Mallaha is the best known, the stone foundations for round houses have been found. It is already clear that further excavations at Mallaha will indicate a more developed Natufian assemblage than the one we now know.

Most of the finds in the Natufian layer of the Mount Carmel cave were flints. About 80 per cent of these flint tools were microliths made by the regular working of tiny blades into various tools, some having geometric forms. The larger flint tools included backed blades, burins, scrapers, a few arrow points, some larger hacking or picking tools, and one special type. This last was the sickle blade.

We know a sickle blade of flint when we see one, because of a strange polish or sheen which seems to develop on the cutting edge when the blade has been used to cut grasses or grain, or—perhaps—reeds. In the Natufian, we have even found the straight bone handles in which a number of flint sickle blades were set in a line.

There was an industry in ground or pecked stone (that is, abraded not chipped) in the Natufian. This included pestle and mortar fragments, and good whole examples at Mallaha. Some mortars had a deep and narrow hole, and some of the pestles show traces of red ochre. We are not sure that all these mortars and pestles were also used for grinding food. In addition, some of the ground stone objects have decorative carving.

NATUFIAN ANTIQUITIES IN OTHER MATERIALS; BURIALS AND PEOPLE

The Natufian industry in bone was quite rich. It included, beside the sickle hafts mentioned above, points and harpoons, straight and curved types of fish-hooks, awls, pins and needles, and a variety of beads and pendants. There were also beads and pendants of pierced teeth and shell.

A number of Natufian burials have been found; some burials were grouped together in one grave. The people who were buried within the Mount Carmel cave were laid on their backs in an extended position, while those on the terrace seem to have been "flexed" (placed in their graves in a curled-up position). This may mean no more than that it was easier to dig a long hole in cave dirt than in the hard-packed dirt of the terrace. The people often had some kind of object buried

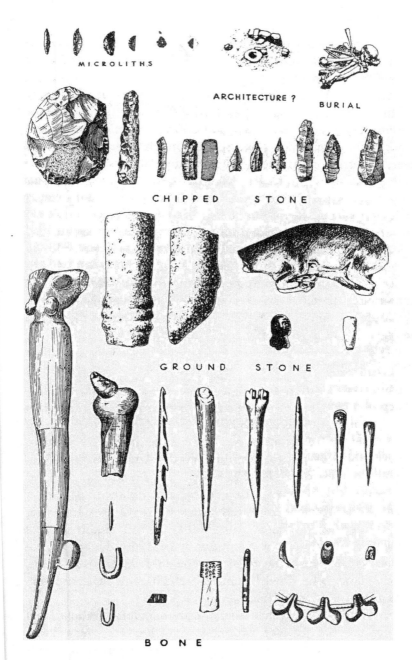

MICROLITHS

ARCHITECTURE ?

BURIAL

CHIPPED STONE

GROUND STONE

BONE

SKETCH OF NATUFIAN ASSEMBLAGE

with them, and several of the best collections of beads come from the burials. On two of the skulls there were traces of elaborate head-dresses of shell beads.

The animal bones of the Natufian layers show beasts of a "modern" type, but with some differences from those of present-day Palestine. The bones of the gazelle outnumber those of the deer; since gazelles like a much drier climate than deer, Palestine must then have had much the same climate that it has today. Some of the animal bones were those of large or dangerous beasts: the hyena, the bear, the wild boar, and the leopard. A domesticated Natufian dog has been reported, but this is questionable. Nor are there yet other *clear* evidences of domesticated animals or plants. It seems likely that the Natufian may have begun as early as about 8000 b.c.

The study of the human bones from the Natufian burials is not yet complete. Until Professor McCown's study becomes available, we may note Professor Coon's assessment that these people were of a "basically Mediterranean type."

THE KARIM SHAHIR ASSEMBLAGE

Karim Shahir differs from Natufian cave sites in that it also shows traces of a temporary open site or encampment. It lies on top of a bluff in the Kurdish hill-country of northeastern Iraq. It was dug by Dr. Bruce Howe of the expedition I directed in 1950–51 for the Oriental Institute and the American Schools of Oriental Research. In 1954–55, our expedition located another site, M'lefaat, with general resemblance to Karim Shahir, but about a hundred miles north of it. In 1956, Dr. Ralph Solecki located still another Karim Shahir type of site called Zawi Chemi Shanidar. In 1960, Howe dug a further site of the same general type in Iranian Kurdistan, Tepe Asiab. The Zawi Chemi site has a radiocarbon determination of 8900 ± 300 b.c.

Karim Shahir has evidence of only one very shallow level of occupation. It was probably not lived on very long, although the people who lived on it spread out over about three acres of area. In spots, the single layer yielded great numbers of fist-sized cracked pieces of limestone, which had been carried up from the bed of a stream at the bottom of the

CHIPPED   STONE

GROUND   STONE

UNBAKED CLAY

SHELL

BONE

"ARCHITECTURE"

SKETCH OF KARIM SHAHIR ASSEMBLAGE

bluff. We think these cracked stones had something to do with a kind of architecture, but we were unable to find positive traces of hut plans. At M'lefaat and Zawi Chemi, there were traces of rounded hut plans, and at Asiab the traces of a large round depression were found.

As in the Natufian, the great bulk of small objects of the Karim Shahir assemblage was in chipped flint. A large proportion of the flint tools were microlithic bladelets and geometric forms. The flint sickle blade was almost non-existent, being far scarcer than in the Natufian. The people of Karim Shahir did a modest amount of work in the grinding of stone; there were milling stone fragments of both the mortar and the quern type, and stone hoes or axes with polished bits. Beads, pendants, rings, and bracelets were made of finer quality stone. We found a few simple points and needles of bone, and even two rather formless unbaked clay figurines which seemed to be of animal form. Zawi Chemi yielded several well made crescent-shaped bone knives with flint blades.

The Karim Shahir phase has not yet yielded direct evidence of the kind of vegetable food its people ate. The animal bones showed a considerable increase in the proportion of the bones of the species capable of domestication—sheep, goat, cattle, horse, dog—as compared with animal bones from the earlier cave sites of the area, which have a high proportion of bones of wild forms like deer and gazelle. There is also increasing evidence that the sheep of Zawi Chemi were actually domesticated; others may also have been, but we have no means at the moment that will tell us from the bones alone.

In 1962, Dr. Frank Hole made a brief preliminary excavation at Ali Kosh, a site low in the Persian foothills overlooking the Mesopotamian plain. Ali Kosh seems to include levels of Karim Shahir type. Hole is now returning for full excavations on this very promising site in a new and lower environmental situation.

WERE THE NATUFIAN AND KARIM SHAHIR PEOPLES FOOD-PRODUCERS?

It is clear that a great part of the food of the Natufian people must have been hunted or collected. Shells of land, fresh-water, and sea animals occur in their cave layers. The same is true as regards the Karim Shahir type sites, save for sea shells. At Asiab, which is beside a river, there were great quantities of river clam shells. But on the other hand, we have the sickles, the milling stones, the Zawi Chemi sheep, and the general animal situation at Karim Shahir to hint at an incipient approach to food-production. In the Karim Shahir type sites, there was the tendency to settle down out in the open; this is echoed by the new open air Natufian sites. The number of stone foundations certainly indicates that it was worth the peoples' while to have some kind of structure, even if the site as a whole was short-lived.

It is a part of my hunch that these things all point toward food-production—that the hints we seek are there. But in the sense that the peoples of the era of the primary village-farming community, which we shall look at next, are fully food-producing, the Natufian and Karim Shahir folk had not yet arrived. I think they were part of a general build-up to full scale food-production. They were possibly controlling a few animals of several kinds and perhaps one or two plants, without realizing the full possibilities of this "control" as a new way of life. I wish I could say whether they were living in their simple settlements all year around or not; some of our evidence seems to point toward seasonal occupation only.

. This is why I think of the Karim Shahir and Natufian folk as being at a level, or in an era, of incipient cultivation and domestication. But we shall have to do a great deal more excavation in this range of time before we'll get the kind of positive information we need.

SUMMARY

I am sorry that this chapter has had to be so much more about ideas than about the archeological traces of prehistoric men themselves. But the antiquities of the incipient era of cultivation and animal domestication will not be spectacular, even when we do have them excavated in quantity. Few museums will be interested in these antiquities for exhibition purposes. The charred bits or impressions of plants, the fragments of animal bone and shell, and the varied clues to climate and environment will be as important as the artifacts themselves. It will be the ideas to which these traces lead us that will be important. I am sure that this unspectacular material—when we have much more of it, and learn how to understand what it says—will lead us to how and why answers about the first great change in human history.

We know the earliest village-farming communities appeared in western Asia, in a nuclear area. We do not yet know why the Near Eastern experiment came first, or why it didn't happen earlier in some other nuclear area. Apparently, the level of culture and the promise of the natural environment were ready first in western Asia. Not by very much, however—the same level appears to have gotten under way in Mesoamerica at least by 7000 B.C. The next sites we look at in the Near East will show a simple but effective food-production already in existence. Without effective food-production and the settled village-farming communities, civilization never could have followed. How effective food-production came into being by the end of the incipient era, is, I believe, one of the most fascinating questions any archeologist could face.

It now seems probable—from possibly two of the Palestinian sites with derived varieties of the Natufian (Jericho and Nahal Oren)—that there were one or more local Palestinian developments out of the Natufian into later times. In the same way, what followed after the Karim Shahir type of assemblage in Iraqi and Iranian Kurdistan was in some ways a reflection of beginnings made at Karim Shahir, Zawi Chemi and Asiab.

THE First Revolution

As the incipient era of cultivation and animal domestication passed onward into the era of the primary village-farming community, the first basic change in human economy was fully achieved. In southwestern Asia, this seems to have taken place about nine thousand years ago. I am going to restrict my description to this earliest Near Eastern case—I do not know enough about the later comparable experiments in the Far East and in the New World. Let us first, once again, think of the contrast between food-collecting and food-producing as ways of life.

THE DIFFERENCE BETWEEN FOOD-COLLECTORS AND FOOD-PRODUCERS

Childe used the word "revolution" because of the radical change that took place in the habits and customs of man. Food-collectors—that is, hunters, fishers, berry- and nut-gatherers—had to live in small groups or bands, for they had to be ready to move wherever their food supply moved. Not many people can be fed in this way in one area, and small children and old folks are a burden. There is not enough food to store, and it is not the kind that can be stored for long.

Do you see how this all fits into a picture? Small groups of people living now in this cave, now in that—or out in the open—as they moved after the animals they hunted; no permanent villages, a few half-buried huts at best; no breakable utensils; no pottery; no signs of anything for clothing beyond the tools that were probably used to dress the skins of animals; no time to think of much of anything but food and protection and disposal of the dead when death did come; an existence which takes nature as it finds it, which does little or nothing to modify nature—all in all, a savage's existence, and a very tough one. A man who spends his whole life following animals just to kill them to eat, or moving from one berry patch to another, is really living just like an animal himself.

THE FOOD-PRODUCING ECONOMY

Against this picture let me try to draw another—that of man's life after food-production had begun. His meat was stored "on the hoof," his grain in silos or great pottery jars. He lived in a house; it was worth his while to build one, because he couldn't move far from his fields and flocks. In his neighborhood enough food could be grown and enough animals bred so that many people were kept busy. They all lived close to their flocks and fields, in a village. The village was already of a fair size, and it was growing, too. Everybody had more to eat; they were presumably all stronger, and there were more children. Children and old men could shepherd the animals by day or help with the lighter work in the fields. After the crops had been harvested the younger men might go hunting and some of them would fish, but the food they brought in was only an addition to the food in the village; the villagers wouldn't starve, even if the hunters and fishermen came home empty-handed.

There was more time to do different things, too. They began to modify nature. They made pottery out of raw clay, and textiles out of hair or fiber. People who became good at pottery-making traded their pots for food and spent all of their time on pottery alone. Other people were learning to weave cloth or to make new tools. There were already people in the village who were becoming full-time craftsmen.

Other things were changing, too. The villagers must have had to agree on new rules for living together. The head man of the village had problems different from those of the chief of the small food-collectors' band. If somebody's flock of sheep spoiled a wheat field, the owner wanted payment for the grain he lost. The chief of the hunters was never bothered with such questions. Even the gods had changed. The spirits and the magic that had been used by hunters weren't of any use to the villagers. They needed gods who would watch over the fields and the flocks, and they eventually began to erect buildings where their gods might dwell, and where the men who knew most about the gods might live.

WAS FOOD-PRODUCTION A "REVOLUTION"?

If you can see the difference between these two pictures—between life in the food-collecting stage and life after food-production had begun—you'll see why Professor Childe spoke of a revolution. By revolution, he did not mean that it happened over night or that it happened only once. We don't know exactly how long it took. Some people think that all these changes may have occurred in less than 500 years, but I doubt that. The incipient era was probably an affair of some duration. Once the level of the village-farming community had been established, however, things did begin to move very fast. By six thousand years ago, the descendants of the first villagers had developed plow agriculture in the relatively rainless Mesopotamian alluvium and were living in towns with temples. Relative to the million years of food-gathering which lay behind, this had been achieved with truly revolutionary suddenness.

GAPS IN OUR KNOWLEDGE OF THE
NEAR EAST

If you'll look again at the chart (p. 111) you'll see that I have few sites and assemblages to name in the incipient era of cultivation and domestication, and not many in the earlier part of the primary village-farming level either. Thanks in no small part to the intelligent co-operation given foreign excavators by the Iraqi and Iranian government antiquities services, our understanding of the sequence in these countries is growing more complete. I shall use them as my main yardstick here. But I am far from being able to show you a series of Sears Roebuck catalogues, even century by century, for any part of the nuclear area. There is still a great deal of earth to move, and a great mass of material to recover and interpret before we even begin to understand "how" and "why."

Perhaps here, because this kind of archeology is really my specialty, you'll excuse it if I become personal for a moment. I very much look forward to having further part in closing some of the gaps in knowledge of the Near East. This is not, as I've told you, the spectacular range of Near Eastern archeology. There are no royal tombs, no gold, no great buildings or sculpture, no writing, in fact nothing to excite the normal museum at all. Nevertheless it is a range which, idea-wise, gives the archeologist tremendous satisfaction. The country of the hilly flanks is an exciting combination of green grasslands and mountainous ridges. The Kurds, who inhabit the part of the area in which I've worked most recently, are an extremely interesting and hospitable people. Archeologists don't become rich, but I'll forego the Cadillac for any bright spring morning in the Kurdish hills, on a good site with a happy crew of workmen and an interested and efficient staff. It is probably impossible to convey the full feeling which life on such a dig holds—halcyon days for the body and acute pleasurable stimulation for the mind. Old things coming newly out of the good dirt, and the pieces of the human puzzle fitting into place! I think I am an honest man; I cannot tell you that I am sorry the job is not yet finished and that there are still gaps in this part of the Near Eastern archeological sequence.

EARLIEST SITES OF THE VILLAGE FARMERS

So far, the Karim Shahir type of assemblage, which we looked at in the last chapter, is the earliest material available in what

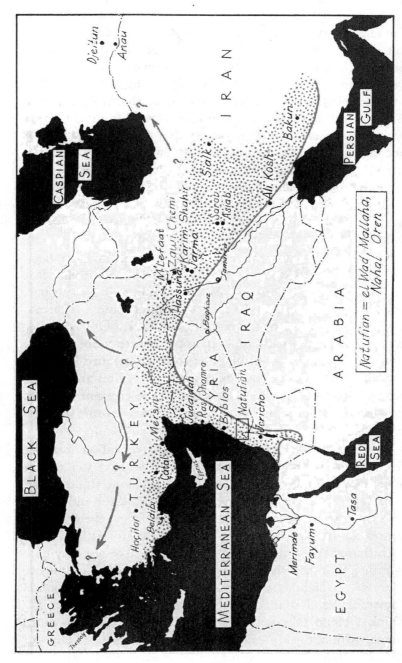

THE NATURAL HABITAT ZONE ABOUT THE CRESCENT AND EARLY SITES OF THE NEAR EAST

I take to be the nuclear area. We do not believe that Karim Shahir was a village site proper; it looks more like the traces of a temporary encampment. Two caves, called Belt and Hotu, which are outside the nuclear area and down on the coastal strip of the Caspian Sea, have been excavated by Professor Coon. These probably belong in the later extension of the terminal era of food-collecting; in their upper layers are traits like the use of pottery borrowed from the more developed era of the same time in the nuclear area. The same general explanation doubtless holds true for certain materials in Egypt, along the upper Nile and in the Kharga oasis: these materials, called Sebilian III, the Khartoum "neolithic," and the Khargan microlithic, are from surface sites, not from caves. The chart (p. 111) shows where I would place these materials in era and time.

M'lefaat, Zawi Chemi, and Asiab appear to have been slightly more "settled in" than was Karim Shahir itself. But I do not think they belong to the era of farming-villages proper. The first site of this era, in the hills of Iraqi Kurdistan, is Jarmo, on which we have spent three seasons of work. Our new site, Sarab, in Iranian Kurdistan, is an approximate counterpart of Jarmo, although its assemblage is somewhat more fully developed. Following Jarmo comes a variety of sites and assemblages which lie along the hilly flanks of the crescent and just below it. I am going to describe and illustrate some of these for you.

Since not very much archeological excavation has yet been done on sites of this range of time, I shall have to mention the names of certain single sites which now alone stand for an assemblage. This does not mean that I think the individual sites I mention were unique. In the times when their various cultures flourished, there must have been many little villages which shared the same general assemblage. We are only now beginning to locate them again. Thus, if I speak of Jarmo, or Jericho, or Sialk as single examples of their particular kinds of assemblages, I don't mean that they were unique at all. I think I could take you to the sites of at least three more Jarmos, within twenty miles of the original one. They are there, but they simply haven't yet been excavated. In 1956, a Danish expedition discovered material of Jarmo type at Shimshara, only two dozen miles northeast of Jarmo, and below (hence sealed in by and earlier than) an assemblage of Hassunan type, which I shall describe presently.

THE GAP BETWEEN KARIM SHAHIR AND JARMO

As we see the matter now, there is probably still a gap in the available archeological record between the Karim Shahir–M'lefaat–Zawi Chemi group (of the incipient era) and that of Jarmo (of the village-farming era). Although some items of the Jarmo type materials do reflect the beginnings of traditions set in the Karim Shahir group (see p. 120), there is not a clear continuity. Moreover—to the degree that we may trust a few radiocarbon determinations—there would appear to be around two thousand years of difference in time. The single available Zawi Chemi "date" is 8900 ± 300 B.C.; the most reasonable group of "dates" from Jarmo averages about 6750 ± 200 B.C.

We shall be on firmer ground when more determinations become available, including those on samples from Asiab. The available Sarab determinations cluster just earlier than 6000 B.C.

JARMO, IN THE KURDISH HILLS, IRAQ

The site of Jarmo has a depth of deposit of about twenty-seven feet, and approximately a dozen layers of architectural renovation and change. Nevertheless it is a "one period" site; its assemblage remains essentially the same throughout, although there are developments in some categories of artifacts and one or two new items are added in later levels. The site covers about four acres of the top of a bluff, below which runs a small stream. It lies in the hill country east of the modern oil town of Kirkuk. The Iraq Directorate General of Antiquities suggested that we look at it in 1948, and we have had three seasons of digging on it since.

The people of Jarmo grew the barley plant and two different kinds of wheat. They made flint sickles with which to reap their grain, mortars or querns on which to crack it, ovens in which it might be parched, and stone bowls out of which they might eat their porridge. We know that they had domesticated goats and sheep, and pigs in the latest levels, but Professor Reed (the staff zoologist) is not convinced that the bones of the other potentially domesticable animals of Jarmo—cattle, horse, dog—show sure signs of domestication. We had first thought that all of these animals were domesticated ones, but Reed feels he must find out much more before he can be sure. As well as their grain and the meat from their animals, the people of Jarmo consumed great quantities of land snails. Botanically, the Jarmo wheat stands about half way between fully bred wheat and the wild forms.

ARCHITECTURE: HALL-MARK OF THE VILLAGE

The sure sign of the village proper is in its traces of architectural permanence. The houses of Jarmo were only the size of a small cottage by our standards, but each was provided with several rectangular rooms. The walls of the houses were made of puddled mud, often set on crude foundations of stone. (The puddled mud wall, which the Arabs call *touf*, is built by laying a three to six inch course of soft mud, letting this sun-dry for a day or two, then adding the next course, etc.) The village probably looked much like the simple Kurdish farming village of today, with its mud-walled houses and low mud-on-brush roofs. I doubt that the Jarmo village had more than twenty houses at any one moment of its existence. Today, an average of about seven people live in a comparable Kurdish house; probably the population of Jarmo was about 150 people.

It is interesting that portable pottery does not appear until the last third of the life of the Jarmo village. Throughout the duration of the village, however, its people had experimented with the plastic qualities of clay. They modeled little figurines of animals and of human beings in clay; one type of human figurine they favored was that of a markedly pregnant woman, probably the expression of some sort of fertility spirit. They provided their house floors with baked-in-place depressions, either as basins or hearths, and later with domed ovens of

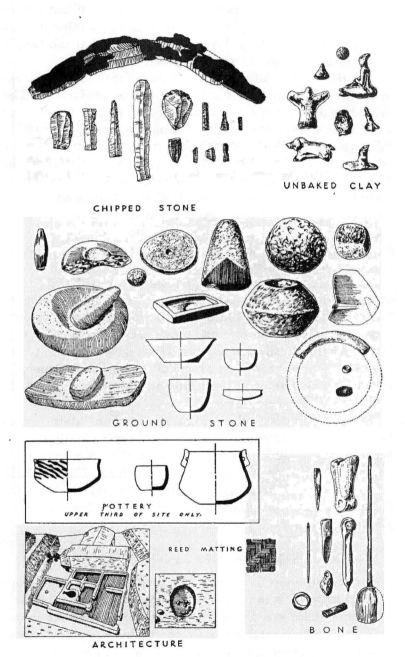

CHIPPED STONE

UNBAKED CLAY

GROUND STONE

POTTERY
UPPER THIRD OF SITE ONLY.

REED MATTING

ARCHITECTURE

BONE

SKETCH OF JARMO ASSEMBLAGE

clay. As we've noted, the houses themselves were of clay or mud; one could almost say they were built up like a house-sized pot. Then, finally, the idea of making portable pottery itself appeared, although I very much doubt that the people of the Jarmo village discovered the art.

On the other hand, the old tradition of making flint blades and microlithic tools was still very strong at Jarmo. The sickle-blade was made in quantities, but so also were many of the much older tool types. Strangely enough, it is within this age-old category of chipped stone tools that we see one of the clearest pointers to a newer age. Many of the Jarmo chipped stone tools—microliths—were made of obsidian, a black volcanic natural glass. The obsidian beds nearest to Jarmo are over three hundred miles to the north. Already a bulk carrying trade had been established—the forerunner of commerce—and the routes were set by which, in later times, the metal trade was to move.

Curiously, our new Jarmo-like site in Iran, Sarab, lacks some of the very items which make Jarmo appear settled. Sarab has the flint and obsidian of Jarmo type, also pottery, clay figurines, stone bowls, and bracelets, even goats and sheep. But its architectural traces are of wretched reed huts at best. It would seem to have been a form of temporary settlement—perhaps for shepherds in the spring and summer. Its inhabitants did have wheat, however.

There are now twelve radioactive carbon "dates" from Jarmo. The most reasonable cluster of determinations averages to about 6750 ± 200 B.C., although there is a completely unreasonable range of "dates" running from 3250 to 9250 B.C.! *If* I am right in what I take to be "reasonable," the first flush of the food-producing revolution had been achieved almost nine thousand years ago.

HASSUNA, IN UPPER MESOPOTAMIAN IRAQ

We are not sure just how soon after Jarmo the next assemblage of Iraqi material is to be placed. I do not think the time was long, and there are a few hints that detailed habits in the making of pottery and ground stone tools were actually continued from Jarmo times into the time of the next full assemblage. This is called after a site named Hassuna, a few miles to the south and west of modern Mosul. We also have Hassunan type materials from several other sites in the same general region. It is probably too soon to make generalizations about it, but the Hassunan sites seem to cluster at slightly lower elevations than those we have been talking about so far.

The catalogue of the Hassuna assemblage is of course more full and elaborate than that of Jarmo. The Iraqi government's archeologists who dug Hassuna itself, exposed evidence of increasing architectural know-how. The walls of houses were still formed of puddled mud; sun-dried bricks appear only in later periods. There were now several different ways of making and decorating pottery vessels. One style of pottery painting, called the Samarran style, is an extremely handsome one and must have required a great deal of concentration and excellence of draftsmanship. On the other hand, the old habits for the preparation of good chipped stone tools—still apparent at Jarmo—seem to have largely disappeared by Hassunan times. The flint work of the Hassunan catalogue is, by and large, a wretched affair. We might guess that the kinaesthetic concentration of the Hassuna craftsmen now went into other categories; that is, they suddenly discovered they might have more fun working with the newer materials. It's a shame that none of their weaving, for example, is preserved for us.

The two available radiocarbon determinations from Hassunan contexts stand at about 5100 and 5600 B.C. ± 250 years.

OTHER EARLY VILLAGE SITES IN THE NUCLEAR AREA

I'll now name and very briefly describe a few of the other early village assemblages either in or adjacent to the hilly flanks of the crescent. Unfortunately, we do not have radioactive carbon dates for many of these materials. We may guess that some particular assemblage, roughly comparable to that of Hassuna, for example, must reflect a culture which existed at about the same time as that of Hassuna. We do this guessing on the basis of the general similarity and degree of

POTTERY

POTTERY OBJECTS

CHIPPED STONE

BONE

GROUND STONE

ARCHITECTURE   REED MATTING   BURIAL

SKETCH OF HASSUNA ASSEMBLAGE

complexity of the Sears Roebuck catalogues of the particular assemblage and that of Hassuna. We suppose that for sites near at hand and of a comparable cultural level, as indicated by their generally similar assemblages, the dating must be about the same. We also know that in a general stratigraphic sense, the sites in question may both appear at the bottom of the ascending village sequence in their respective areas. Without a number of consistent radioactive carbon dates, we cannot be precise about priorities.

The ancient mound called Tell es-Sultan at Jericho, in the Dead Sea valley in Palestine, yields some very interesting material. Its catalogue somewhat resembles that of Jarmo, especially in the sense that there is a fair depth of deposit without portable pottery vessels. On the other hand, the architecture of Tell es-Sultan is surprisingly complex, with traces of massive stone fortification walls and the general use of formed sun-dried mud brick. Jericho lies in a somewhat strange and tropically lush ecological niche, some seven hundred feet below sea level; it is geographically within the hilly-flanks zone but environmentally not part of it.

Several radiocarbon "dates" for Tell es-Sultan fall in the range of those I find reasonable for Jarmo, and their internal statistical consistency is far better than that for the Jarmo determinations. It is not clear at this time exactly what this means.

Tell es-Sultan contains a remarkably fine sequence, which perhaps does not have the gap we noted in Iraqi-Kurdistan between the Karim Shahir group and Jarmo. While I am not sure that this sequence will prove valid for those parts of Palestine outside the special Dead Sea environmental niche, the sequence does appear to proceed from the local variety of Natufian into that of a very well-settled community. So far, we have little direct evidence for the food-production basis upon which the Tell es-Sultan people subsisted, save for the presence of domesticated goats.

There is an early village assemblage with strong characteristics of its own in the land bordering the northeast corner of the Mediterranean Sea, where Syria and the Cilician province of Turkey join. This early Syro-Cilician assemblage must represent a general cultural pattern which was at least in part contemporary with that of the Hassuna assemblage. At the base of the coastal site of Ras Shamra, a pre-ceramic phase of the assemblage is reported. The materials from the bases of the mounds at Mersin, and from Judaidah in the Amouq plain, as well as from a few other sites, represent the remains of true villages. The walls of their houses were built of puddled mud, but some of the house foundations were of stone. Several different kinds of pottery were made by the people of these villages. None of it resembles the pottery from Hassuna or from the upper levels of Jarmo or Jericho. The Syro-Cilician people had not lost their touch at working flint. An important southern variation of the Syro-Cilician assemblage has been cleared recently at Byblos, a port town famous in later Phoenician times. There are three radiocarbon determinations which suggest that the time range for these developments was probably in the late seventh to early sixth millennium B.C.

Another important new sequence, with pre-ceramic basal layers, is now being tested in south central Turkey. At Haçilar, near Burdur lake, we have radiocarbon determinations for the layers with pottery and fine figurines (above the basal layers) at about 5500 B.C. According to the excavator, Mr. James Mellaart, the gap between the pre-ceramic and the ceramic layers of Haçilar is to be seen at the site of Çatal Hüyük (hüyük = mound). Çatal has yielded a very well-built village, whose house-walls were decorated with remarkable mural paintings. Perhaps this sequence is still another development, not connected with Jarmo, Jericho, or the Syro-Cilician one; more likely, it was loosely related to that of Syro-Cilicia. Still more pre-ceramic horizons, on sites in Cyprus and in Thessaly in northern Greece, await their place as our ideas of the general scheme develop. Professor V. Milojcic's site of Gremnos-Argissa in Thessaly appears to be without pottery. An important new site in Macedonia, which does have pottery, is Nea Nikomedeia, with a single radiocarbon determination of about 6250 B.C. ± 150 years. An equally early pre-ceramic village has even been reported from Crete.

THE IRANIAN PLATEAU AND THE NILE VALLEY

The map on page 125 shows some sites which lie either outside or in an extension of the natural habitat zone proper. From the base of the great mound at Sialk on the Iranian plateau came an assemblage of early village material, generally similar, in the kinds of things it contained, to the catalogues of Hassuna and Judaidah. The details of how things were made are different; the Sialk assemblage represents still another cultural pattern. I suspect it appeared a bit later in time than did that of Hassuna. There is an important new item in the Sialk catalogue. The Sialk people made small drills or pins of hammered copper. Thus the metallurgist's specialized craft had made its appearance.

There is at least one very early Iranian site on the inward slopes of the hilly-flanks zone. It is the earlier of two mounds at a place called Bakun, in southwestern Iran; the results of the excavations there are not yet published and we only know of its coarse and primitive pottery. I only mention Bakun because it may yet help us to delimit the natural habitat zone villages on the map.

The Nile Valley lies beyond the peculiar environmental zone flanking the crescent, and it is probable that the earliest village-farming communities in Egypt were established by a few people who wandered into the Nile delta area from the nuclear area. The assemblage which is most closely comparable to the catalogue of Hassuna or Judaidah, for example, is that from little settlements along the shore of the Fayum lake. The Fayum materials come mainly from grain bins or silos. Another site, Merimde, in the western part of the Nile delta, shows the remains of a true village, but it may be slightly later than the settlement of the Fayum. There are radioactive carbon "dates" for the Fayum materials at about 4275 B.C. and from Merimde at about 4100 B.C., which is almost fifteen hundred years later than the determinations suggested for the Hassunan or Syro-Cilician assemblages. I suspect that this is a somewhat over-extended indication of the time it took for the generalized cultural pattern of village-farming community life to spread from the nuclear area down into Egypt, but as yet we have no way of testing these matters.

In this same vein, we have two radioactive carbon determinations for an assemblage from sites near Khartoum in the
Sudan, best represented by the mound called Shaheinab. The
Shaheinab catalogue roughly corresponds to that of the Fayum;
the distance between the two places, as the Nile flows, is roughly
1,500 miles. Thus it took almost a thousand years for the
new way of life to be carried as far south into Africa as Khartoum; the two Shaheinab "dates" average about 3300 B.C.
± 400 years.

If the movement was up the Nile (southward), as these
dates suggest, then I suspect that the earliest available village
material of middle Egypt, the so-called Tasian, is also later
than that of the Fayum. The Tasian materials come from
a few graves near a village called Deir Tasa, and I have
an uncomfortable feeling that the Tasian "assemblage" may
be mainly an artificial selection of poor examples of objects
which belong in the following range of time.

SPREAD IN TIME AND SPACE

There are now two things we can do; in fact, we have already
begun to do them. We can watch the spread of the new way
of life upward through time in the nuclear area. We can also
see how the new way of life spread outward in space from the
nuclear area, as time went on. There is good archeological
evidence that both these processes took place. For the hill
country of northeastern Iraq, in the nuclear area, we have
already noticed how the succession (still with gaps) from
Karim Shahir, through M'lefaat and Jarmo, to Hassuna can
be charted (see chart, p. 111). In the next chapter, we shall
continue this charting and description of what happened in
Iraq upward through time. We also watched traces of the
new way of life move through space up the Nile into Africa,
to reach Khartoum in the Sudan some thirty-five hundred
years later than we had seen it at Jarmo or Jericho. We
caught glimpses of it in the Fayum and perhaps at Tasa along
the way.

For the remainder of this chapter, I shall try to suggest
briefly for you the directions taken by the spread of the new
way of life from the nuclear area in the Near East. First, let

me make clear again that I *do not* believe that the village-farming community way of life was invented only once and in the Near East. It seems to me that the evidence is very clear that a separate experiment arose in the New World. For China, the question of independence or borrowing—in the appearance of the village-farming community there—is still an open one. In the last chapter, we noted the probability of an independent nuclear area in southeastern Asia. Professor Carl Sauer strongly champions the great importance of this area as *the* original center of agricultural pursuits, as a kind of "cradle" of all incipient eras of the Old World at least. While there is certainly not the slightest archeological evidence to allow us to go that far, we may easily expect that an early southeast Asian development would have been felt in China. However, the appearance of the village-farming community in the northwest of India, or at least as we now know it, seems to have depended on the earlier development in the Near East. It is also probable that ideas of the new way of life moved well beyond Khartoum in Africa.

THE SPREAD OF THE VILLAGE-FARMING COMMUNITY WAY OF LIFE INTO EUROPE

How about Europe? I won't give you many details. You can easily imagine that the late prehistoric prelude to European history is a complicated affair. We all know very well how complicated an area Europe is now, with its welter of different languages and cultures. Remember, however, that a great deal of archeology has been done on the late prehistory of Europe, and very little on that of further Asia and Africa. If we knew as much about these areas as we do of Europe, I expect we'd find them just as complicated.

This much is clear for Europe, as far as the spread of the village-community way of life is concerned. The general idea and much of the know-how and the basic tools of food-production moved from the Near East to Europe. So did the plants and animals which had been domesticated; they were not naturally at home in Europe, as they were in western Asia. I do not, of course, mean that there were traveling salesmen who carried these ideas and things to Europe with a commercial gleam in their eyes. The process took time, and the ideas and things must have been passed on from one group of people to the next. There was also some actual movement of peoples, but we don't know the size of the groups that moved.

The story of the "colonization" of Europe by the first farmers is thus one of (1) the movement from the eastern Mediterranean lands of some people who were farmers; (2) the spread of ideas and things beyond the Near East itself and beyond the paths along which the "colonists" moved; and (3) the adaptations of the ideas and things by the indigenous Forest folk, about whose "receptiveness" Professor Mathiassen speaks (p. 97). It is important to note that the resulting cultures in the new European environment were European, not Near Eastern. The late Professor Childe remarked that "the peoples of the West were not slavish imitators; they adapted the gifts from the East . . . into a new and organic whole capable of developing on its own original lines."

THE WAYS TO EUROPE

Suppose we want to follow the traces of those earliest village-farmers who did travel from western Asia into Europe. Let us start from Syro-Cilicia, that part of the hilly-flanks zone proper which lies in the very northeastern corner of the Mediterranean. Three ways would be open to us (of course we could not be worried about permission from the Soviet authorities!). We would go north, or north and slightly east, across Anatolian Turkey, and skirt along either shore of the Black Sea or even to the east of the Caucasus Mountains along either flank of the Caspian Sea, to reach Ukrainian Russia. From here, we could march across eastern Europe to the Baltic and Scandinavia, or even hook back southwestward to Atlantic Europe.

Our second way from Syro-Cilicia would also lie over Anatolia, perhaps past the Haçilar site, to the northwest, where we would have to swim or raft ourselves over the Dardanelles or the Bosphorus to the European shore. Then we could bear left toward Thessaly in Greece. But some of us might turn right again in Macedonia, going up the valley

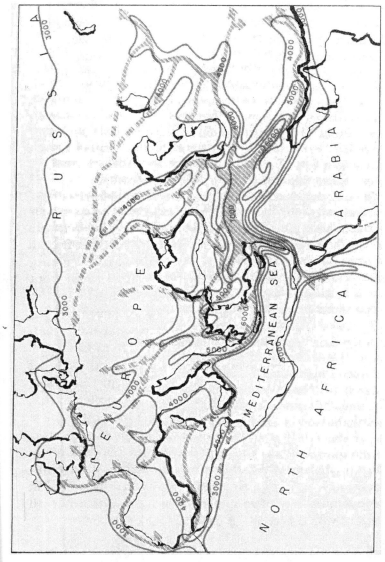

POSSIBLE ROUTES AND TIMING IN THE SPREAD OF THE VILLAGE-FARMING COMMUNITY
WAY OF LIFE FROM THE NEAR EAST TO EUROPE

Based on speculations derived from the now available radiocarbon determinations at sites rather randomly
distributed over the entire area

of the Vardar River to its divide and on down the valley of the Morava beyond, to reach the Danube near Belgrade in Jugoslavia. Here we would turn left, following the great river valley of the Danube up into central Europe. We would have a number of tributary valleys to explore, or we could cross the divide and go down the valley of the Rhine to the North Sea.

Our third way from Syro-Cilicia would be by sea. We would coast along southern Anatolia and visit Cyprus, Crete, and the Aegean islands on our way to Greece, where, in the north, we might meet some of those who had taken the second route. From Greece, we would sail on to Italy and the western isles, to reach southern France and the coasts of Spain. Eventually a few of us would sail up the Atlantic coast of Europe, to reach western Britain and even Ireland.

Of course none of us could ever take these journeys as the first farmers took them, since the whole course of each journey must have lasted many lifetimes. The radiocarbon determinations for the earliest farmers of the Rhine delta in Holland run at about 4200 B.C. Somewhere before 6000 B.C. might be a safe date to give for the well-developed early village communities of Syro-Cilicia. We suspect that the spread throughout Europe did not proceed at an even rate. Nevertheless, it would appear as if the new way of life was making itself felt along the Atlantic seaboard of Europe, somewhat more than two thousand years after it was established in Syro-Cilicia.

I offer a highly speculative attempt at charting this spread on a map with isochronic or time contour lines (p. 139). The map actually assumes that village-farming communities had been established in the natural habitat zone in southwestern Asia by about 7000 B.C. We do not know just how soon after this the spread began, but it must have been under way by 6000 B.C. Using the still rather few radiocarbon determinations we now have, I have sketched the way in which I think the time contours may have spread. I warn you that not all prehistorians would accept the implications of this map.

THE EARLIEST FARMERS OF ENGLAND

To describe the later prehistory of all Europe for you would take another book and a much larger one than this is. There-

fore, I have decided to give you only a few impressions of the later prehistory of Britain. Of course the British Isles lie at the other end of Europe from our base-line in western Asia. Also, they received influences along at least two of the three ways in which the new way of life moved into Europe. We will look at more of their late prehistory in a following chapter: here, I shall speak only of the first British farmers we now know.

The earliest known British artifacts implying farming are already said to be "mature" and to have an "insular and distinctive character." This assemblage, called Windmill Hill, which appears in the south and southeast of England, exhibits three different kinds of structures, evidence of grain-growing and of stock-breeding, and some distinctive types of pottery and stone implements. Some of these materials may date as early as 3500 B.C. The most remarkable type of structure is the earthwork enclosures which some authorities believe may have served as seasonal cattle corrals. These enclosures were roughly circular, reached over a thousand feet in diameter, and sometimes included two or three concentric sets of banks and ditches. Traces of oblong timber houses have been found, but not within the enclosures. The second type of structure is mine-shafts, dug down into the chalk beds where good flint for the making of axes or hoes could be found. The third type of structure is long simple mounds or "unchambered barrows," in one end of which burials were made. Professor Piggott believes that the Windmill Hill materials embody a mixture of traditions from more than one continental European source. The so-called Chassey tradition in France is considered to be one source. Another source—more difficult to identify—lay in the geographical region of the Low Countries and the north European plain.

The archeological traces of a second early culture are to be found in the west of England, western and northern Scotland, and most of Ireland. The bearers of this culture had come up the Atlantic coast by sea from southern France and Spain. The evidence they have left us consists mainly of tombs and the contents of tombs, with only very rare settlement sites. The tombs were of some size and received the bodies of many people. The tombs themselves were built of

stones, heaped over with earth; the stones enclosed a passage to a central chamber ("passage graves"), or to a simple long gallery, along the sides of which the bodies were laid ("gallery graves"). The general type of construction is called "megalithic" (= great stone), and the whole earth-mounded structure is often called a *barrow*. Since many have proper chambers, in one sense or another, we used the term "unchambered barrow" above to distinguish those of the Windmill Hill type from these megalithic structures. There is some evidence for sacrifice, libations, and ceremonial fires, and it is clear that some form of community ritual was focused on the megalithic tombs.

The cultures of the people who produced the Windmill Hill assemblage and of those who made the megalithic tombs flourished, at least in part, at the same time. Although the distributions of the two different types of archeological traces are in quite different parts of the country, there is Windmill Hill pottery in some of the megalithic tombs. But the tombs also contain pottery which is not of standard Windmill Hill type, although it need not necessarily be considered to be foreign in origin.

A third early British group of antiquities of this time (following soon after 3000 B.C. at the latest) comes from sites in southern and eastern England. It is not certain that the people who made this generalized assemblage were farmers. While they may on occasion have practiced a simple agriculture, many items of their assemblage link them closely with that of the "Forest folk" of earlier times in England and in the Baltic countries. In fact, Professor Piggott has favored the term "Secondary Neolithic cultures" (which not all authorities accept) as a descriptive handle for these generalized materials that appear to be the result of the acceptance—by indigenous food-collectors—of some food-producing ways of making and doing things. Some of the pottery, originally called the Peterborough type, is decorated with impressions of cords and was at first believed to be quite different from that of Windmill Hill and the megalithic builders. It is now taken to be an insular evolution of earlier Windmill Hill types. In addition, the distribution of these finds extends into eastern Britain,

where the other cultures have left no trace. The makers of this assemblage had villages with semi-subterranean huts, and the bones of oxen, pigs, and sheep have been found in a few of these. On the whole, however, hunting and fishing seem to have been their vital occupations. They also established trade routes especially to acquire the raw material for stone axes.

A probably slightly later culture, whose traces are best known from Skara Brae on Orkney, also had its roots in those cultures of the Baltic area which fused out of the meeting of the Forest folk and the peoples who took the eastern way into Europe. Skara Brae is very well preserved, having been built of thin stone slabs about which dune-sand drifted after the village died. The individual houses, the bedsteads, the shelves, the chests for clothes and oddments—all built of thin stone slabs—may still be seen in place. But the Skara Brae people lived entirely by sheep- and cattle-breeding, and by catching shellfish. Neither grain nor the instruments of agriculture appeared at Skara Brae.

THE EUROPEAN ACHIEVEMENT

The above is only a very brief description of what went on in Britain with the arrival of the first farmers. There are many interesting details which I have omitted in order to shorten the story.

I believe some of the difficulty we have in understanding the establishment of the first farming communities in Europe is with the word "colonization." We have a natural tendency to think of "colonization" as it has happened within the last few centuries. In the case of the colonization of the Americas, for example, the colonists came relatively quickly, and in increasingly vast numbers. They had vastly superior technical, political, and war-making skills, compared with those of the Indians. There was not much mixing with the Indians. The case in Europe five or six thousand years ago must have been very different. I wonder if it is even proper to call people "colonists" who move some miles to a new region, settle down and farm it for some years, then move on again, generation after generation? The ideas and the things which these new people carried were only *potentially* superior. The ideas and things and the people had to prove themselves in their adaptation to each new environment. Once this was done another link to the chain would be added, and then the forest-dwellers and other indigenous folk of Europe along the way might accept the new ideas and things. It is quite reasonable to expect that there must have been much mixture of the migrants and the indigenes along the way; each of the assemblages we mentioned above would seem to show more or less clear traces of such fused cultures. Sometimes, especially if the migrants were moving by boat, long distances may have been covered in a short time. Remember, however, we seem to have almost three thousand years between the early Syro-Cilician villages and Windmill Hill.

Let me repeat Professor Childe again. "The peoples of the West were not slavish imitators: they adapted the gifts from the East . . . into a new and organic whole capable of developing on its own original lines." Childe is of course completely conscious of the fact that his "peoples of the West" were in part the descendants of migrants who came originally from the "East," bringing their "gifts" with them. This was the late prehistoric achievement of Europe—to take new ideas and things and some migrant peoples and, by mixing them with the old in its own environments, to forge a new and unique series of cultures.

What we know of the ways of men suggests to us that when the details of the later prehistory of further Asia and Africa are learned, their stories will be just as exciting.

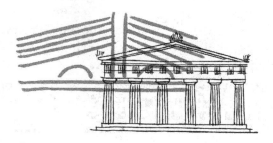

THE Conquest of Civilization

Now we must return to the Near East again. We are coming to the point where history is about to begin. I am going to stick pretty close to Iraq and Egypt in this chapter. These countries will perhaps be the most interesting to most of us, for the foundations of western civilization were laid in the river lands of the Tigris and Euphrates and of the Nile. I shall probably stick closest of all to Iraq, because things first happened there and also because I know it best.

There is another interesting thing, too. We have seen that the first experiment in village-farming took place in the Near East. So did the first experiment in civilization. Both experiments "took." The traditions we live by today are based, ultimately, on those ancient beginnings in food-production and civilization in the Near East.

WHAT "CIVILIZATION" MEANS

I shall not try to define "civilization" for you; rather, I shall tell you what the word brings to my mind. To me civilization means urbanization: the fact that there are cities. It means a formal political set-up—that there are kings or governing bodies that the people have set up. It means formal laws—rules of conduct—which the government (if not the

people) believes are necessary. It probably mea.
are formalized projects—roads, harbors, irrigation ﹢
the like—and also some sort of army or police force *here
them. It means quite new and different art forms. ᧚
usually means there is writing. (The people of the An.
the Incas—had everything which goes to make up a c﹍
ization but formal writing. I can see no reason to say th﹍
were not civilized.) Finally, as the late Professor Redfield﹍
reminded us, civilization seems to bring with it the dawn of
a new kind of moral order.

In different civilizations, there may be important differences in the way such things as the above are managed. In
early civilizations, it is usual to find religion very closely tied
in with government, law, and so forth. The king may also be
a high priest, or he may even be thought of as a god. The
laws are usually thought to have been given to the people by
the gods. The temples are protected just as carefully as the
other projects.

CIVILIZATION IMPOSSIBLE WITHOUT
FOOD-PRODUCTION

Civilizations have to be made up of many people. Some of
the people live in the country; some live in very large towns or
cities. Classes of society have begun. There are officials and
government people; there are priests or religious officials;
there are merchants and traders; there are craftsmen, metal-
workers, potters, builders, and so on; there are also farmers,
and these are the people who produce the food for the whole
population. It must be obvious that civilization cannot exist
without food-production and that food-production must also
be at a pretty efficient level of village-farming before civilization can even begin.

But people can be food-producing without being civilized.
In many parts of the world this is still the case. When the
white men first came to America, the Indians in most parts
of this hemisphere were food-producers. They grew corn,
potatoes, tomatoes, squash, and many other things the white
men had never eaten before. But only the Aztecs of Mexico,

the Mayas of Yucatan and Guatemala, and the Incas of the Andes were civilized.

WHY DIDN'T CIVILIZATION COME TO ALL FOOD-PRODUCERS?

Once you have food-production, even at the well-advanced level of the village-farming community, what else has to happen before you get civilization? Many men have asked this question and have failed to give a full and satisfactory answer. There is probably no *one* answer. We can make an "informed guess" as to one of the reasons why civilization *may* have come about in the Near East alone. Remember, it is only a guess—a putting together of hunches from incomplete evidence. It is *not* necessarily meant to explain how civilization began in any of the other areas—China, southeast Asia, the Americas—where other early experiments in civilization went on. The details in those areas are quite different. Whether certain general principles hold for the appearance of any early civilization is still an open and very interesting question.

WHERE CIVILIZATION FIRST APPEARED IN THE NEAR EAST

You remember that our earliest village-farming communities lay along the hilly flanks of a great "crescent" and in valley plains above this "crescent." (See map on p. 125.) Professor Breasted's "fertile crescent" emphasized the lower and richer valleys of the Nile and the Tigris-Euphrates Rivers. Our hilly-flanks area of the crescent zone arches up from Egypt through Palestine and Syria, along southern Turkey into northern Iraq, and down along the southwestern fringe of Iran. The earliest food-producing villages of which we have knowledge already existed in this area by about 6750 B.C. (± 200 years).

Now notice that this hilly-flanks zone does not include southern Mesopotamia, the alluvial land of the lower Tigris and Euphrates in Iraq, or the Nile Valley proper. The earliest known villages of classic Mesopotamia and Egypt seem to appear fifteen hundred or more years after those of the hilly-flanks zone. For example, the early Fayum village which lies near a lake west of the Nile Valley proper (see p. 135) has a radiocarbon date of 4275 B.C. ± 320 years. It was in the river lands, however, that the immediate beginnings of civilization were made.

We know that by about 3200 B.C. the Early Dynastic period had begun in southern Mesopotamia. The beginnings of writing go back several hundred years earlier, but we can safely say that civilization had begun in Mesopotamia by 3200 B.C. In Egypt, the beginning of the First Dynasty is slightly later, at about 3100 B.C., and writing probably did not appear much earlier. Some authorities have understood the chronological evidence to favor later dates (by about 200 years in each case) for the beginnings of civilization in both Egypt and Mesopotamia. The now available radiocarbon determinations seem to support this lower chronology. But—in round numbers—we may still say that history and civilization were well under way in both Mesopotamia and Egypt by 3000 B.C. —about five thousand years ago.

THE HILLY-FLANKS ZONE VERSUS THE RIVER LANDS

Why did these two civilizations spring up in these two river lands which apparently were not even part of the area where the village-farming community began? Why didn't we have the first civilizations in southern Turkey, Syria, Palestine, north Iraq, or Iran, where we're sure food-production had had a long time to develop? I think the probable answer gives a clue to the ways in which civilization began in Egypt and Mesopotamia.

The land in the hilly flanks and in the mountain valley plains beyond is of a sort which people can farm without too much trouble. There is a fairly fertile coastal strip in Palestine and Syria. There are pleasant mountain slopes, streams running out to the sea, and rain, at least in the winter months. The rain belt and the foothills of the Turkish mountains also extend to northern Iraq and on to the Iranian plateau. The Iranian plateau has its mountain valleys, streams, and some rain. These hilly flanks of the "crescent," through most of its arc, are almost made-to-order for beginning farmers. The grassy slopes of the higher hills would be pasture for their herds and flocks. As soon as the earliest experiments with agriculture and domestic animals had been successful, a pleasant living could be made—and without too much trouble.

I should add here again, that our evidence points increasingly to a climate for those times which is very little different from that for the area today.

THE RIVER LANDS

Now look at Egypt and southern Mesopotamia. Both are lands without rain, for all intents and purposes. Both are lands with rivers that have laid down very fertile soil—soil perhaps superior to that in the hilly flanks. But in both lands, the rivers are of no great aid without some control.

The Nile floods its banks once a year, in late September or early October. It not only soaks the narrow fertile strip of land on either side; it lays down a fresh layer of new soil each year. Beyond the fertile strip on either side rise great cliffs, and behind them is the desert. In its natural, uncontrolled state, the yearly flood of the Nile must have caused short-lived swamps that were full of crocodiles. After a short time, the flood level would have dropped, the water and the crocodiles would have run back into the river, and the swamp plants would have become parched and dry.

The Tigris and the Euphrates of Mesopotamia are less likely to flood regularly than the Nile. The Tigris has a shorter and straighter course than the Euphrates; it is also the more violent river. Its banks are high, and when the snows melt and flow into all of its tributary rivers it is swift and dangerous. The Euphrates has a much longer and more curving course and few important tributaries. Its banks are lower and it is less likely to flood dangerously. The land on either side and between the two rivers is very fertile, south of the modern city of Baghdad. Unlike the Nile Valley, neither the Tigris nor the Euphrates is flanked by cliffs. The land on either side of the rivers stretches out for miles and is not much rougher than a poor tennis court.

THE RIVERS MUST BE CONTROLLED

The real trick in both Egypt and Mesopotamia is to make the rivers work for you. In Egypt, this is a matter of building dikes and reservoirs that will catch and hold the Nile flood. In this way, the water is held and allowed to run off over the fields as it is needed. In Mesopotamia, it is a matter of taking advantage of natural river channels and branch channels, and of leading ditches from these onto the fields.

Obviously, we can no longer find the first dikes or reservoirs of the Nile Valley, or the first canals or ditches of Mesopotamia. The same land has been lived on far too long for any traces of the first attempts to be left; or, especially in Egypt, it has been covered by the yearly deposits of silt, dropped by the river floods. But we're pretty sure the first food-producers of Egypt and southern Mesopotamia must have made such dikes, canals, and ditches. In the first place, there can't normally have been enough rain for them to grow things otherwise. In the second place, the patterns for such projects seem to have been pretty well set by historic times.

CONTROL OF THE RIVERS THE BUSINESS
OF EVERYONE

Here, then, is probably a *part* of the reason why civilization grew in Egypt and Mesopotamia first—not in Palestine, Syria, or Iran. In the latter areas, people could produce their food as individuals. It wasn't too hard; there were rain and some streams, and good pasturage for the animals even if a crop or two went wrong. In Egypt and Mesopotamia, people had to put in a much greater amount of work, and this work couldn't be individual work. Whole villages or groups of people had to turn out to fix dikes or dig ditches. The dikes had to be repaired and the ditches carefully cleared of silt each year, or they would become useless.

There also had to be hard and fast rules. The person who lived nearest the ditch or the reservoir must not be allowed to take all the water and leave none for his neighbors. It was not only a business of learning to control the rivers and of making their waters do the farmer's work. It also meant controlling men. But once these men had managed both kinds of controls, what a wonderful yield they had! The soil was already fertile, and the silt which came in the floods and ditches kept adding fertile soil.

THE GERM OF CIVILIZATION IN EGYPT AND MESOPOTAMIA

This learning to work together for the common good was the real germ of the Egyptian and the Mesopotamian civilizations. The bare elements of civilization were already there: the need for a governing hand and for laws to see that the communities' work was done and that the water was justly shared. You may object that there is a sort of chicken and egg paradox in this idea. How could the people set up the rules until they had managed to get a way to live, and how could they manage to get a way to live until they had set up the rules? I think that small groups must have moved down along the mud-flats of the river banks quite early, making use of naturally favorable spots, and that the rules grew out of such cases. It would have been like the hand-in-hand growth of automobiles and paved highways in the United States.

Once the rules and the know-how did get going, there must have been a constant interplay of the two. Thus, the more the crops yielded, the richer and better-fed the people would have been, and the more the population would have grown. As the population grew, more land would have needed to be flooded or irrigated, and more complex systems of dikes, reservoirs, canals, and ditches would have been built. The more complex the system, the more necessity for work on new projects and for the control of their use . . . . And so on . . . .

What I have just put down for you is a guess at the manner of growth of some of the formalized systems that go to make up a civilized society. My explanation has been pointed particularly at Egypt and Mesopotamia. The canalization and water-control part of it does not apply nearly so clearly to the development of the Aztecs or at all to the Mayas. But I think that a fair part of the story of Egypt and Mesopotamia must be as I've just told you.

I am particularly anxious that you do *not* understand me to mean that canalization *caused* civilization. I am sure it was not that simple at all. For, in fact, a complex and highly engineered irrigation system proper did not come until later times. Let's say rather that the simple beginnings of irrigation allowed and in fact encouraged a great number of things in the technological, political, social, and moral realms of culture. Another factor of importance—as the population grew larger and the variety of needs of the society tended to encourage more specialization—must have been a gradual shift of peoples' interests and loyalties from their relatives or kin-group to the group of specialists to which they belonged. Simple villages tended to have their interests focused on what the kin-group considered to be most important. In cities, such loyalties and interests tended to be less purely kin-oriented. We do not yet understand what all these things were or how they worked. But without these other aspects of culture, I do not think that urbanization and civilization itself could have come into being.

THE ARCHEOLOGICAL SEQUENCE TO CIVILIZATION IN IRAQ

We last spoke of the archeological materials of Iraq on page 130, where I described the village-farming community of Hassunan type. The Hassunan type villages appear in the hilly-flanks zone and in the rolling land adjacent to the Tigris in northern Iraq. It is probable that even before the Hassuna pattern of culture lived its course, a new assemblage had been established in northern Iraq and Syria. This assemblage is called Halaf, after a site high on a tributary of the Euphrates, on the Syro-Turkish border. There is a single radiocarbon determination for the Halafian at about 5750 B.C.

The Halafian assemblage is incompletely known. The culture it represents included a remarkably handsome painted pottery. Archeologists have tended to be so fascinated with this pottery that they have bothered little with the rest of the Halafian assemblage. We do know that strange stone-founded houses, with plans like those of the popular notion of an Eskimo igloo, were built. Like the pottery of the Samarran style, which appears as part of the Hassunan assemblage (see p. 131), the Halafian painted pottery implies great concentration and excellence of draftsmanship on the part of the people who painted it.

We must mention two very interesting sites adjacent to the mud-flats of the rivers, half way down from northern Iraq to the classic alluvial Mesopotamian area. One is Baghouz on the Euphrates, the other is Samarra on the Tigris (see map,

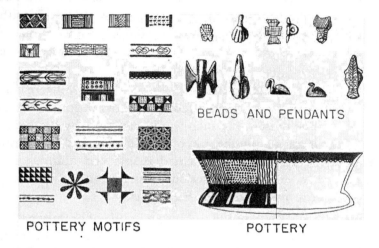

BEADS AND PENDANTS

POTTERY MOTIFS   POTTERY

SKETCH OF SELECTED ITEMS OF HALAFIAN ASSEMBLAGE

p. 125). Both these sites yield the handsome painted pottery of the style called Samarran; in fact it is Samarra which gives its name to the pottery. Neither Baghouz nor Samarra has completely Hassunan types of assemblages, and at Samarra there are a few pots of proper Halafian style. I suppose that Samarra and Baghouz give us glimpses of those early farmers who had begun to finger their way down the mud-flats of the river-banks toward the fertile but yet untilled southland. Not all of the new ideas need have entered classic Mesopotamia from the north, however. Some doubtless came from Khuzestan, immediately to the east. There were doubtless also river-bank food-collectors living in southern Mesopotamia long before ideas of a village-farming community way of life ever reached the area.

Our next step is into the southland proper. Here, deep in the core of the mound which later became the holy Sumerian city of Eridu, Iraqi archeologists uncovered a handsome painted pottery. This "Eridu" pottery, which is about all we have of the assemblage of the people who once produced it, may be seen as a blend of the Samarran and Halafian painted pottery styles. This may over-simplify the case, but as yet we do not have much evidence to go on. The idea does at least fit with my interpretation of the meaning of Baghouz and Samarra as way-points on the mud-flats of the rivers half way down from the north.

My colleague, Robert Adams, believes that there were certainly earlier riverine-adapted food-collectors in lower Mesopotamia. The presence of such would explain why the Eridu assemblage is not simply the sum of the Halafian and Samarran assemblages. But the domesticated plants and animals and the basic ways of food-production must have come from the hilly-flanks country in the north and east.

Above the basal Eridu levels comes a style of pottery called Haji Mohammed, first found by German excavators near Warka and quite recently by the British near Baghdad. Then —as at a number of other sites in the south—comes a full-fledged assemblage called Ubaid. Incidentally, there is an aspect of the Ubaidian assemblage in the north as well. It seems to move into place before the Halaf manifestation is finished, and to blend with it. The Ubaidian assemblage in the south is by far the more spectacular. The development of the temple has been traced at Eridu from a simple little structure to a monumental building some 62 feet long, with a pilaster-decorated façade and an altar in its central chamber. There is painted Ubaidian pottery, but the style is hurried and somewhat careless and gives the *impression* of having been a cheap mass-production means of decoration when compared with the carefully drafted styles of Samarra and Halaf or with the basal Eriduan or Haji Mohammed pottery. The Ubaidian people made other items of baked clay: sickles and axes of very

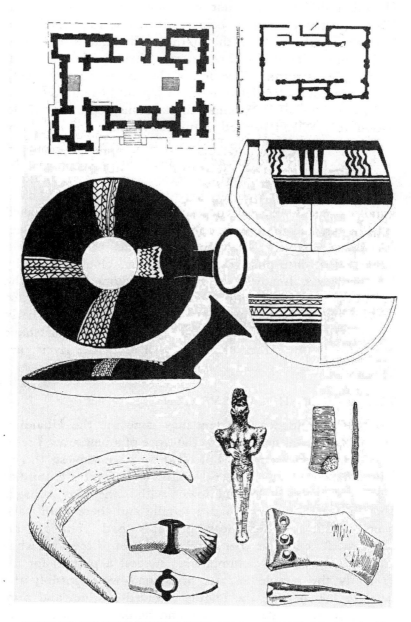

SKETCH OF SELECTED ITEMS OF UBAIDIAN ASSEMBLAGE

hard-baked clay are found. The northern Ubaidian sites have yielded tools of copper, but metal tools of unquestionable Ubaidian find-spots are not yet available from the south. Clay figurines of human beings with monstrous turtle-like faces are another item in the southern Ubaidian assemblage.

There is a large Ubaid cemetery at Eridu, much of it still awaiting excavation. The few skeletons so far tentatively studied reveal a completely modern type of "Mediterraneanoid"; the individuals whom the skeletons represent would undoubtedly blend perfectly into the modern population of southern Iraq. What the Ubaidian assemblage says to us is that these people had already adapted themselves and their culture to the peculiar riverine environment of classic southern Mesopotamia. For example, hard-baked clay axes will chop bundles of reeds very well, or help a mason dress his unbaked mud bricks, and there were only a few soft and pithy species of trees available. The Ubaidian levels of Eridu yield quantities of date pits; that excellent and characteristically Iraqi fruit was already in use. The excavators also found the clay model of a ship, with the stepping-point for a mast, so that Sinbad the Sailor must have had his antecedents as early as the time of Ubaid. The bones of fish, which must have flourished in the larger canals as well as in the rivers, are common in the Ubaidian levels and thereafter.

THE UBAIDIAN ACHIEVEMENT

On present evidence, my tendency is to see the Ubaidian assemblage in southern Iraq as the trace of a new era. I wish there were more evidence, but what we have suggests this to me. The culture of southern Ubaid soon became a culture of towns—of centrally located towns with some rural villages about them. The town had a temple and there must have been priests. These priests probably had political and economic functions as well as religious ones, if the somewhat later history of Mesopotamia may suggest a pattern for us. Presently the temple and its priesthood were possibly the focus of the market; the temple received its due, and may already have had its own lands and herds and flocks. The people of the town, undoubtedly at least in consultation with the temple administration, planned and maintained the simple irrigation ditches. As the system flourished, the community of rural farmers would have produced more than sufficient food. The tendency for specialized crafts to develop—tentative at best at the cultural level of the earlier village-farming community era—would now have been achieved, and probably many other specialists in temple administration, water control, architecture, and trade would also have appeared, as the surplus food-supply was assured.

Southern Mesopotamia is not a land rich in natural resources other than its fertile soil. Stone, good wood for construction, metal, and innumerable other things would have had to be imported. Grain and dates—although both are bulky and difficult to transport—and wool and woven stuffs must have been the mediums of exchange. Over what area did the trading net-work of Ubaid extend? We start with the idea that the Ubaidian assemblage is most richly developed in the south. We assume, I think, correctly, that it represents a cultural flowering of the south. On the basis of the pottery of the still elusive "Eridu" immigrants who had first followed the rivers into alluvial Mesopotamia, we get the notion that the characteristic painted pottery style of Ubaid was developed in the southland. If this reconstruction is correct then we may watch with interest where the Ubaid pottery-painting tradition spread. We have already mentioned that there is a substantial assemblage of (and from the southern point of view, *fairly* pure) Ubaidian material in northern Iraq. The pottery appears all along the Iranian flanks, even well east of the head of the Persian Gulf, and ends in a later and spectacular flourish in an extremely handsome painted style called the "Susa" style. Ubaidian pottery has been noted up the valleys of both of the great rivers, well north of the Iraqi and Syrian borders on the southern flanks of the Anatolian plateau. It reaches the Mediterranean Sea and the valley of the Orontes in Syria, and it may be faintly reflected in the painted style of a site called Ghassul, on the east bank of the Jordan in the Dead Sea Valley. Over this vast area—certainly in all of the great basin of the Tigris–Euphrates drainage system and its natural extensions—I believe we may lay our fingers on the traces of a peculiar way of decorating pottery, which we call Ubaidian. This cursive and even slap-dash decoration, it appears to me, was part of a new cultural tradition which arose from the adjustments which immigrant northern farmers first made to the new and challenging environment of southern Mesopotamia. But exciting as the idea of the spread of influences of the Ubaid tradition in space may be, I believe you will agree that the consequences of the growth of that tradition in southern Mesopotamia itself, as time passed, are even more important.

THE WARKA PHASE IN THE SOUTH

So far, there are only two radiocarbon determinations for the Ubaidian assemblage, one from Tepe Gawra in the north and one from Warka in the south. My hunch would be to use the dates 4500 to 3750 B.C., with a plus or more probably a minus factor of about two hundred years for each, as the time duration of the Ubaidian assemblage in southern Mesopotamia.

Next, much to our annoyance, we have what is almost a temporary black-out. According to the system of terminology I favor, our next "assemblage" after that of Ubaid is called the *Warka* phase, from the Arabic name for the site of Uruk or Erich. We know it only from six or seven levels in a narrow test-pit at Warka, and from an even smaller hole at another site. This "assemblage," so far, is known only by its pottery, some of which still bears Ubaidian style painting. The characteristic Warkan pottery is unpainted, with smoothed red or gray surfaces and peculiar shapes. Unquestionably, there must be a great deal more to say about the Warkan assemblage, but someone will first have to excavate it!

THE DAWN OF CIVILIZATION

After our exasperation with the almost unknown Warka interlude, following the brilliant "false dawn" of Ubaid, we move next to an assemblage which yields traces of a preponderance of those elements which we noted (p. 145) as meaning civilization. This assemblage is that called *Proto-Literate:* it already contains writing. On the somewhat shaky principle that writing, however early, means history—and no longer prehistory—the assemblage is named for the historical implications of its content, and no longer after the name of the site where it was first found. Since some of the older books used site-names for this assemblage, I will tell you that the Proto-Literate includes the latter half of what used to be called the "Uruk period" *plus* all of what used to be called the "Jemdet Nasr period." It shows a consistent development from beginning to end.

I shall, in fact, leave much of the description and the historic implications of the Proto-Literate assemblage to the conventional historians. Professor T. J. Jacobsen, reaching backward from the legends he finds in the cuneiform writings of slightly later times, can in fact tell you a more complete story of Proto-Literate culture than I can. It should be enough here if I sum up briefly what the excavated archeological evidence shows.

We have yet to dig a Proto-Literate site in its entirety, but the indications are that the sites cover areas the size of small cities. In architecture, we know of large and monumental temple structures, which were built on elaborate high terraces. The plans and decoration of these temples follow the pattern set in the Ubaid phase; the chief difference is one of size. The German excavators at the site of Warka reckoned that the construction of only one of the Proto-Literate temple complexes there must have taken 1,500 men, each working a ten-hour day, five years to build.

ART AND WRITING

If the architecture, even in its monumental forms, can be seen to stem from Ubaidian developments, this is not so with our other evidence of Proto-Literate artistic expression. In relief and applied sculpture, in sculpture in the round, and on the engraved cylinder seals—all of which now make their appearance,—several completely new artistic principles are apparent. These include the composition of subject-matter in groups, commemorative scenes, and especially the ability and ap-

RELIEF ON A PROTO-LITERATE STONE VASE, WARKA
Unrolled drawing, with restoration suggested by figures from
contemporary cylinder seals

parent desire to render the human form and face. Excellent
as the animals of the Franco-Cantabrian art may have been
(see p. 85), and however handsome were the carefully drafted
geometric designs and conventionalized figures on the pottery
of the early farmers, there seems to have been, up to this time,
a mental block about the drawing of the human figure and
especially the human face. We do not yet know what caused
this self-consciousness about picturing themselves which
seems characteristic of men before the appearance of civilization. We do know that with civilization, the mental block
seems to have been removed.

Clay tablets bearing pictographic signs are the Proto-
Literate forerunners of cuneiform writing. The earliest examples are not well understood but they seem to be "devices

for making accounts and for remembering accounts." Different from the later case in Egypt, where writing appears fully formed in the earliest examples, the development from simple pictographic signs to proper cuneiform writing may be traced, step by step, in Mesopotamia. It is most probable that the development of writing was connected with the temple and the need for keeping account of the temple's possessions. Professor Jacobsen sees writing as a means for overcoming space, time, and the increasing complications of human affairs: "Literacy, which began with . . . civilization, enhanced mightily those very tendencies in its development which characterize it as a civilization and mark it off as such from other types of culture."

While the new principles in art and the idea of writing are not foreshadowed in the Ubaid phase, or in what little we know of the Warkan, I do not think we need to look outside southern Mesopotamia for their beginnings. We do know something of the adjacent areas, too, and these beginnings are not there. I think we must accept them as completely new discoveries, made by the people who were developing the whole new culture pattern of classic southern Mesopotamia.

THE PROTO-LITERATE ACHIEVEMENT

Full description of the art, architecture, and writing of the Proto-Literate phase would call for many details. Men like Professors Jacobsen and Adams can give you these details much better than I can. Nor shall I do more than tell you that the common pottery of the Proto-Literate phase was so well standardized that it looks factory made. There was also some handsome painted pottery, and there were stone bowls with inlaid decoration. Well-made tools in metal had by now become fairly common, and the metallurgist was experimenting with the casting process. Signs for plows have been identified in the early pictographs, and a wheeled chariot is shown on a cylinder seal engraving. But if I were forced to a guess in the matter, I would say that the development of plows and draft-animals probably began in the Ubaid period and was another of the great innovations of that time.

The Proto-Literate assemblage clearly suggests a highly developed and sophisticated culture. While perhaps not yet fully urban, it is on the threshold of urbanization. There seems to have been a very dense settlement of Proto-Literate sites in classic southern Mesopotamia, many of them newly founded on virgin soil where no earlier settlements had been. When we think for a moment of what all this implies, of the growth of a canalization system which must have existed to allow the flourish of this culture, and of the social and political organization necessary to maintain the canals, I think we will agree that at last we are dealing with civilization proper.

FROM PREHISTORY TO HISTORY

Now it is time for the conventional ancient historians to take over the story from me. Remember this when you read what they write. Their real base-line is with cultures ruled over by later kings and emperors, whose writings describe military campaigns and the administration of laws and fully organized trading ventures. To these historians, the Proto-Literate phase is still a simple beginning for what is to follow. If they mention the Ubaid assemblage at all—the one I was so lyrical about—it will be as some dim and fumbling step on the path to the civilized way of life.

I suppose you could say that the difference in the approach is that as a prehistorian I have been looking forward or upward in time, while the historians look backward to glimpse what I've been describing here. My base-line was a million or more years ago with a being who had little more than the capacity to make tools and fire to distinguish him from the animals about him. Thus my point of view and that of the conventional historian are bound to be different. You will need both if you want to understand all of the story of men, as they lived through time to the present.

End of PREHISTORY

You'll doubtless easily recall your general course in ancient history: how the Sumerian dynasties of Mesopotamia were supplanted by those of Babylonia, how the Hittite kingdom appeared in Anatolian Turkey, and about the three great phases of Egyptian history. The literate kingdom of Crete arose, and by 1500 B.C. there were splendid fortified Mycenean towns on the mainland of Greece. This was the time—about the whole eastern end of the Mediterranean—of what Professor Breasted called the "first great internationalism," with flourishing trade, international treaties, and royal marriages between Egyptians, Babylonians, and Hittites. By 1200 B.C., the whole thing had fragmented; "the peoples of the sea were restless in their isles," and the great ancient centers in Egypt, Mesopotamia, and Anatolia were eclipsed. Numerous smaller states arose—Assyria, Phoenicia, Israel—and the Trojan war was fought. Finally Assyria became the paramount power of all the Near East, presently to be replaced by Persia.

A new culture, partaking of older west Asiatic and Egyptian elements, but casting them with its own tradition into a new mould, arose in mainland Greece and along the Ionian coast of Anatolia.

I once shocked my Classical colleagues to the core by referring to Greece as "a second degree derived civilization," but there is much truth in this. The principles of bronze- and then of iron-working, of the alphabet, and of many other elements in Greek culture were borrowed from western Asia. Our debt to the Greeks is too well known for me even to mention it, beyond recalling to you that it is to Greece we owe the beginnings of rational or empirical science and thought in general. But Greece fell in its turn to Rome, and in 55 B.C. Caesar invaded Britain.

I last spoke of Britain on page 142; I had chosen it as my single example for telling you something of how the earliest farming communities were established in Europe. Now I will continue with Britain's later prehistory, so you may sense something of the end of prehistory itself. Remember that Britain is simply a single example we select; the same thing could be done for all the other countries of Europe, and will be possible also, some day, for further Asia and Africa. Remember, too, that prehistory in most of Europe runs on for three thousand or more years *after* conventional ancient history begins in the Near East. Britain is a good example to use in showing how prehistory ended in Europe. As we said earlier, it lies at the opposite end of Europe from the area of highest cultural achievement in those times, and should you care to read more of the story in detail, you may do so in English.

METAL USERS REACH ENGLAND

We left the story of Britain with the peoples who made several different but perhaps in part related assemblages—the Windmill Hill, the megalith-builders, and Professor Piggott's generalized "Secondary Neolithic cultures"—making adjustments to their environments, to the original inhabitants of the island, and to each other. They had first arrived at least by 3500 B.C., and were simple pastoralists and hoe cultivators who lived in village communities. Some of them planted little if any grain. By 2000 B.C., they were well settled in. Then, somewhere in the range from about 1900 to 1800 B.C., the traces of the invasion of a new series of peoples begin to appear.

The first newcomers are called the Beaker folk, after the name of a peculiar form of pottery they made. The beaker type of pottery seems oldest in Spain, where it occurs with great collective tombs of megalithic construction and with copper tools. But the Beaker folk who reached England seem already to have moved first from Spain(?) to the Rhineland and Holland. While in the Rhineland, and before leaving for England, the Beaker folk seem to have mixed with the local population and also with incomers from northeastern Europe whose culture included elements brought originally from the Near East by the eastern way through the steppes. This last group has also been named for a peculiar article in its assemblage; the group is called the Battle-axe folk. A few Battle-axe folk elements, including, in fact, stone battle-axes, reached England with the earliest Beaker folk,[1] coming from the Rhineland.

The Beaker folk settled earliest in the agriculturally fertile south and east. There seem to have been several phases of Beaker folk invasions, and it is not clear whether these all came strictly from the Rhineland or Holland. We do know that their copper daggers and awls and armlets are more of Irish or Atlantic European than of Rhineland origin. A few simple habitation sites and many burials of the Beaker folk are known. They buried their dead singly, sometimes in conspicuous individual barrows with the dead warrior in his full trappings. The spectacular element in the assemblage of the Beaker folk is a group of large circular monuments with ditches and with uprights of wood or stone. These "henges" became truly monumental several hundred years later; while

[1] The British authors use the term "Beaker folk" to mean both archeological assemblage and human physical type. They speak of a " .... tall, heavy-boned, rugged, and round-headed" strain which they take to have developed, apparently in the Rhineland, by a mixture of the original (Spanish?) beaker-makers and the northeast European battle-axe makers. However, since the science of physical anthropology is very much in flux at the moment, and since I am not able to assess the evidence for these physical types, I *do not* use the term "folk" in this book with its usual meaning of standardized physical type. When I use "folk" here, I mean simply *the makers of a given archeological assemblage.* The difficulty only comes when assemblages are named for some item in them; it is too clumsy to make an adjective of the item and refer to a "beakerian" assemblage.

they were occasionally dedicated with a burial, they were not primarily tombs. The effect of the invasion of the Beaker folk seems to cut across the whole fabric of life in Britain. There is at least a suggestion, however, that the very earliest of the

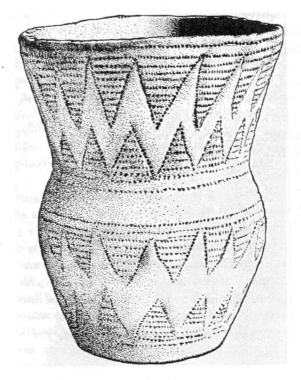

BEAKER

"henges" may have been started during Piggott's "Secondary Neolithic culture" phase.

There was, furthermore, a second major element in British life at this time. It shows itself in the less well understood traces of a group again called after one of the items in their catalogue, the Food-vessel folk. There are many burials in these "food, vessel" pots in northern England, Scotland, and Ireland, and the pottery itself seems to link back to that of the Peterborough type. Like some of the earlier so-called "Secondary Neolithic" people in the highland zone before them, the makers of the food-vessels seem to have been heavily involved in trade. It is quite proper to wonder whether the food-vessel pottery itself was made by local women who were married to traders who were middlemen in the transmission of Irish metal objects to north Germany and Scandinavia. The belt of high, relatively woodless country, from southwest to northeast, was already established as a natural route for inland trade.

MORE INVASIONS

About 1500 B.C., the situation became further complicated by the arrival of new people in the region of southern England anciently called Wessex. The traces suggest the Brittany coast of France as a source, and the people seem at first to have been a small but "heroic" group of aristocrats. Their "heroes" are buried with wealth and ceremony, surrounded by their axes and daggers of bronze, their gold ornaments, and amber and jet beads. These rich finds show that the trade-linkage these warriors patronized spread from the Baltic sources of amber to Mycenean Greece or even Egypt, as evidenced by glazed blue beads.

The great visual trace of Wessex achievement. is the final form of the spectacular sanctuary at Stonehenge. A wooden henge or circular monument was first made several hundred years earlier, but the site now received its great circles of stone uprights and lintels. The diameter of the surrounding ditch at Stonehenge is about 350 feet, the diameter of the inner circle of large stones is about 100 feet, and the tallest stone of the innermost horseshoe-shaped enclosure is 29 feet 8 inches high. One circle is made of blue stones which must have been transported from Pembrokeshire, 145 miles away as the crow flies. Recently, many carvings representing the profile of a standard type of bronze axe of the time, and several profiles of bronze daggers—one of which has been called Mycenean in type— have been found carved in the stones. We cannot, of course, describe the details of the religious ceremonies which must have been staged in Stonehenge, but we can certainly imagine the well-integrated and smoothly working culture which must have been necessary before such a great monument could have been built.

"THIS ENGLAND"

The range from 1900 to about 1400 B.C. includes the time of development of the archeological features usually called the "Early Bronze Age" in Britain. In fact, traces of the Wessex warriors persisted down to about 1200 B.C. The main regions of the island were populated, and the adjustments to the highland and lowland zones were distinct and well marked. The different aspects of the assemblages of the Beaker folk and the clearly expressed activities of the Food-vessel folk and the Wessex warriors show that Britain was already taking on her characteristic trading role, separated from the European continent but conveniently adjacent to it. The tin of Cornwall —so important in the production of good bronze—as well as the copper of the west and of Ireland, taken with the gold of Ireland and the general excellence of Irish metal work, assured Britain a trader's place in the then known world. Contacts with the eastern Mediterranean may have been by sea, with Cornish tin as the attraction, or may have been made by the Food-vessel middlemen on their trips to the Baltic coast. There they would have encountered traders who traveled the great north-south European road, by which Baltic amber moved southward to Greece and the Levant, and ideas and things moved northward again.

There was, however, the Channel between England and Europe, and this relative isolation gave some peace and also gave time for a leveling and further fusion of culture. The separate cultural traditions began to have more in common. The growing of barley, the herding of sheep and cattle, and the production of woollen garments were already features common to all Britain's inhabitants save a few in the remote highlands, the far north, and the distant islands not yet fully touched by food-production. The "personality of Britain" was being formed.

Along with people of certain religious faiths, archeologists are against cremation (for other people!). Individuals to be cremated seem in past times to have been dressed in their trappings and put upon a large pyre; it takes a lot of wood and a very hot fire for a thorough cremation. When the burning had been completed, the few fragile scraps of bone and such odd beads of stone or other rare items as had resisted the great heat seem to have been whisked into a pot and the pot buried. The archeologist is left with the pot and the unsatisfactory scraps in it.

Tentatively, after about 1400 B.C. and almost completely over the whole island by 1200 B.C., Britain became the scene of cremation burials in urns. We know very little of the people themselves. None of their settlements have been identified, although there is evidence that they grew barley and made enclosures for cattle. The urns used for the burials seem to have antecedents in the pottery of the Food-vessel folk, and there are some other links with earlier British traditions. In Lancashire, a wooden circle seems to have been built about a grave with cremated burials in urns. Even occasional instances of cremation may be noticed earlier in Britain, and it is not clear what, if any, connection the British cremation burials in urns have with the classic *Urnfields* which were now beginning in the east Mediterranean and which we shall mention below.

The British cremation-burial-urn folk survived a long time in the highland zone. In the general British scheme, they make up what is called the "Middle Bronze Age," but in the highland zone they last until after 900 B.C. and are considered to be a specialized highland "Late Bronze Age." In the highland zone, these later cremation-burial folk seem to have continued the older Food-vessel tradition of being middlemen in the metal market.

Granting that our knowledge of this phase of British prehistory is very restricted because the cremations have left so little for the archeologist, it does not appear that the cre-

mation-burial-urn folk can be sharply set off from their
immediate predecessors. But change on a grander scale was
on the way.

REVERBERATIONS FROM CENTRAL EUROPE

In the centuries immediately following 1000 B.C., we see with
fair clarity two phases of a cultural process which must have
been going on for some time. Certainly several of the invasions we have already described in this chapter were due to
earlier phases of the same cultural process, but we could not
see the details.

Around 1200 B.C., central Europe was upset by the spread
of the so-called Urnfield folk, who practiced cremation burial
in urns and whom we also know to have been possessors of

SLASHING SWORD

long, slashing swords and the horse. I told you above that we
have no idea that the Urnfield folk proper were in any way
connected with the people who made cremation-burial-urn
cemeteries a century or so earlier in Britain. It has been
supposed that the Urnfield folk themselves may have shared
ideas with the people who sacked Troy. We know that the
Urnfield pressure from central Europe displaced other people
in northern France, and perhaps in northwestern Germany,
and that this reverberated into Britain about 1000 B.C.

Soon after 750 B.C., the same thing happened again. This
time, the pressure from central Europe came from the Hallstatit
folk, who were iron tool makers; the reverberation brought
people from the western Alpine region across the Channel
into Britain.

At first it is possible to see the separate results of these
folk movements, but the developing cultures soon fused with
each other and with earlier British elements. Presently there

were also strains of other northern and western European pottery and traces of Urnfield practices themselves which appeared in the finished British product. I hope you will sense that I am vastly over-simplifying the details.

The result seems to have been—among other things—a new kind of agricultural system. The land was marked off by ditched divisions. Rectangular fields imply the plow rather than hoe cultivation. We seem to get a picture of estate or tribal boundaries which included village communities; we find a variety of tools in bronze, and even whetstones which show that iron has been honed on them (although the scarce iron has not been found). Let me give you the picture in Professor S. Piggott's words: "The . . . Late Bronze Age of southern England was but the forerunner of the earliest Iron Age in the same region, not only in the techniques of agriculture, but almost certainly in terms of ethnic kinship . . . . we can with some assurance talk of the Celts . . . . the great early Celtic expansion of the Continent is recognized to be that of the Urnfield people."

Thus, certainly by 500 B.C., there were people in Britain, some of whose descendants we may recognize today in name or language in remote parts of Wales, Scotland, and the Hebrides.

THE COMING OF IRON

Iron—once the know-how of reducing it from its ore in a very hot, closed fire has been achieved—produces a far cheaper and much more efficient set of tools than does bronze. Iron tools seem first to have been made in quantity in Hittite Anatolia about 1500 B.C. In continental Europe, the earliest, so-called Hallstatt, iron-using cultures appeared in Germany soon after 750 B.C. Somewhat later, Greek and especially Etruscan exports of *objets d'art*—which moved with a flourishing trans-Alpine wine trade—influenced the Hallstatt iron-working tradition. Still later, new classical motifs, together with older Hallstatt, oriental, and northern nomad motifs, gave rise to a new style in metal decoration which characterizes the so-called La Tène phase.

A few iron users reached Britain a little before 400 B.C. Not long after that, a number of allied groups appeared in southern and southeastern England. They came over the Channel from France and must have been Celts with dialects related to those already in England. A second wave of Celts arrived from the Marne district in France about 250 B.C. Finally, in the second quarter of the first century B.C., there were several groups of newcomers, some of whom were Belgae of a mixed Teutonic–Celtic confederacy of tribes in northern France and Belgium. The Belgae preceded the Romans by only a few years.

HILL-FORTS AND FARMS

The earliest iron-users seem to have entrenched themselves temporarily within hill-top forts, mainly in the south. Gradually, they moved inland, establishing *individual* farm sites with extensive systems of rectangular fields.. We recognize these fields by the "lynchets" or lines of soil-creep which plowing left on the slopes of hills. New crops appeared; there were now bread wheat, oats, and rye, as well as barley.

At Little Woodbury, near the town of Salisbury, a farmstead has been rather completely excavated. The rustic buildings were within a palisade, the round house itself was built of wood, and there were various outbuildings and pits for the storage of grain. Weaving was done on the farm, but not blacksmithing, which must have been a specialized trade. Save for the lack of firearms, the place might almost be taken for a farmstead on the American frontier in the early 1800's.

Toward 250 B.C. there seems to have been a hasty attempt to repair the hill-forts and to build new ones, evidently in response to signs of restlessness being shown by remote relatives in France.

THE SECOND PHASE

Perhaps the hill-forts were not entirely effective or perhaps a compromise was reached. In any case, the newcomers from the Marne district did establish themselves, first in the southeast and then to the north and west. They brought iron with decoration of the La Tène type, and also the two-wheeled chariot. Like the Wessex warriors of over a thousand years earlier, they made "heroes' " graves, with their warriors buried in the war-chariots and dressed in full trappings.

CELTIC BUCKLE

The metal work of these Marnian newcomers is excellent. The peculiar Celtic art style, based originally on the classic tendril motif, is colorful and virile, and fits with Greek and Roman descriptions of Celtic love of color in dress. There is a strong trace of these newcomers northward in Yorkshire, linked by Ptolemy's description to the Parisii, doubtless part of the Celtic tribe which originally gave its name to Paris on the Seine. Near Glastonbury, in Somerset, two villages in swamps have been excavated. They seem to date toward the middle of the first century B.C., which was a troubled time in Britain. The circular houses were built on timber platforms surrounded with palisades. The preservation of antiquities by the water-logged peat of the swamp has yielded us a long catalogue of the materials of these villagers.

In Scotland, which yields its first iron tools at a date of about 100 B.C., and in northern Ireland even slightly earlier, the effects of the two phases of newcomers tend especially to blend. Hill-forts, "brochs" (stone-built round towers) and a variety of other strange structures seem to appear as the new ideas develop in the comparative isolation of northern Britain.

THE THIRD PHASE

For the time of about the middle of the first century B.C., we again see traces of frantic hill-fort construction. This simple military architecture now took some new forms. Its multiple ramparts must reflect the use of slings as missiles, rather than spears. We probably know the reason. In 56 B.C., Julius Caesar chastised the Veneti of Brittany for outraging the dignity of Roman ambassadors. The Veneti were famous slingers, and doubtless the reverberations of escaping Veneti were felt across the Channel. The military architecture suggests that some Veneti did escape to Britain.

Also, through Caesar, we learn the names of newcomers who arrived in two waves, about 75 B.C. and about 50 B.C. These were the Belgae. Now, at last, we can even begin to speak of dynasties and individuals. Some time before 55 B.C., the Catuvellauni, originally from the Marne district in France, had possessed themselves of a large part of southeastern England. They evidently sailed up the Thames and built a town of over a hundred acres in area. Here ruled Cassivellaunus, "the first man in England whose name we know," and whose town Caesar sacked. The town sprang up elsewhere again, however.

THE END OF PREHISTORY

Prehistory, strictly speaking, is now over in southern Britain. Claudius' effective invasion took place in 43 A.D.; by 83 A.D., a raid had been made as far north as Aberdeen in Scotland. But by 127 A.D., Hadrian had completed his wall from the Solway to the Tyne, and the Romans settled behind it. In Scotland, Romanization can have affected the countryside very little. Professor Piggott adds that ". . . it is when the pressure of Romanization is relaxed by the break-up of the Dark Ages that we see again the Celtic metal-smiths handling their material with the same consummate skill as they had before the Roman Conquest, and with traditional styles that had not even then forgotten their Marnian and Belgic heritage."

In fact, many centuries go by, in Britain as well as in the rest of Europe, before the archeologist's task is complete and the historian on his own is able to describe the ways of men in the past.

BRITAIN AS A SAMPLE OF THE GENERAL COURSE OF PREHISTORY IN EUROPE

In giving this very brief outline of the later prehistory of Britain, you will have noticed how often I had to refer to the European continent itself. Britain, beyond the English Channel for all of her later prehistory, had a much simpler course of events than did most of the rest of Europe in later prehistoric times. This holds, in spite of all the "invasions" and "reverberations" from the continent. Most of Europe was the scene of an even more complicated ebb and flow of cultural change, save in some of its more remote mountain valleys and peninsulas.

The whole course of later prehistory in Europe is, in fact, so very complicated that there is no single good book to cover it all; certainly there is none in English. There are some good regional accounts and some good general accounts of part of the range from about 3000 B.C. to A.D. 1. I suspect that the difficulty of making a good book that covers all of its later prehistory is another aspect of what makes Europe so very complicated a continent today. The prehistoric foundations for Europe's very complicated set of civilizations, cultures, and sub-cultures—which begin to appear as history proceeds— were in themselves very complicated.

Hence, I selected the case of Britain as a single example of how prehistory ends in Europe. It could have been more complicated than we found it to be. Even in the subject matter on Britain in the chapter before the last, we did not see direct traces of the effect on Britain of the very important developments which took place in the Danubian way from the Near East. Apparently Britain was not affected. Britain received the impulses which brought copper, bronze, and iron tools from an original east Mediterranean homeland into Europe, almost at the ends of their journeys. But by the same token, they had had time en route to take on their characteristic European aspects.

Some time ago, Sir Cyril Fox wrote a famous book called *The Personality of Britain*, sub-titled "Its Influence on Inhabitant and Invader in Prehistoric and Early Historic Times." We have not gone into the post-Roman early historic period here; there are still the Anglo-Saxons and Normans to account for as well as the effects of the Romans. But what I have tried to do was to begin the story of how the personality of Britain was formed. The principles that Fox used, in trying to balance cultural and environmental factors and inter-relationships would not be greatly different for other lands.

Summary OH·UO$_2$·O·I=O I·O·OH

In the pages you have read so far, you have been brought through the earliest 99 per cent of the story of man's life on this planet. I have left only 1 per cent of the story for the historians to tell.

THE DRAMA OF THE PAST

Men first became men when evolution had carried them to a certain point. This was the point where the eye-hand-brain co-ordination was good enough so that tools could be made. When tools began to be made according to sets of lasting habits, we know that men had appeared. This happened less than a million years ago. The stage for the play may have been as broad as all of Europe, Africa, and Asia. At least, it seems unlikely that only one little region saw the beginning of the drama.

Glaciers and different climates came and went, to change the settings. But the play went on in the same first act for a very long time. The men who were the players had simple roles. They had to feed themselves and protect themselves as best they could. They did this by hunting, catching, and finding food wherever they could, and by taking such protection as caves, fire, and their simple tools would give them. Before the first act was over, the last of the glaciers was melting away, and the players had added the New World to their stage. If we want a special name for the first act, we could call it *The Food-Gatherers.*

There were not many climaxes in the first act, so far as we can see. But I think there may have been a few. Certainly the pace of the first act accelerated with the swing from simple gathering to more intensified collecting. The great cave art of France and Spain was probably an expression of a climax. Even the ideas of burying the dead and of the "Venus" figurines must also point to levels of human thought and activity that were over and above pure food-getting.

THE SECOND ACT

The second act began only about ten thousand years ago. A few of the players started it by themselves near the center of the Old World part of the stage, in the Near East. It began as a plant and animal act, but it soon became much more complicated.

But the players in this one part of the stage—in the Near East—were not the only ones to start off on the second act by themselves. Other players, possibly in several places in the Far East, and certainly in the New World, also started second acts that began as plant (and animal) acts, and then became complicated. We can call the whole second act *The Food-Producers.*

THE FIRST GREAT CLIMAX OF THE SECOND ACT

In the Near East, the first marked climax of the second act happened in Mesopotamia and Egypt. The play and the players reached that great climax that we call civilization. This seems to have come less than five thousand years after the second act began. But it could never have happened in the first act at all.

There is another curious thing about the first act. Many of the players didn't know it was over and they kept on with their roles long after the second act had begun. On the edges of the stage there are today some players who are still going on with the first act. The Eskimos, and the native Australians, and certain tribes in the Amazon jungle are some of these players. They seem perfectly happy to keep on with the first act.

The second act moved from climax to climax. The civilizations of Mesopotamia and Egypt were only the earliest of these climaxes. The players to the west caught the spirit of the thing, and climaxes followed there. So also did climaxes come in the Far Eastern and New World portions of the stage.

The greater part of the second act should really be described to you by a historian. Although it was a very short act when compared to the first one, the climaxes complicate it a great deal. I, a prehistorian, have only told you about the first act, and the very beginning of the second.

THE THIRD ACT

Also, as a prehistorian I probably should not even mention the third act—it began so recently. The third act is *The Industrialization*. It is the one in which we ourselves are players. If the pace of the second act was so much faster than that of the first, the pace of the third act is terrific. The danger is that it may wear down the players completely.

What sort of climaxes will the third act have, and are we already in one? You have seen by now that the acts of my play are given in terms of modes or basic patterns of human economy—ways in which people get food and protection and safety. The climaxes involve more than human economy. Economics and technological factors may be part of the climaxes, but they are not all. The climaxes may be revolutions in their own way, intellectual and social revolutions if you like.

If the third act follows the pattern of the second act, a climax should come soon after the act begins. We may be due for one soon if we are not already in it. Remember the terrific pace of this third act.

WHY BOTHER WITH PREHISTORY?

Why do we bother about prehistory? The main reason is that we think it may point to useful ideas for the present. We are in the troublesome beginnings of the third act of the play. The beginnings of the second act may have lessons for us and give depth to our thinking. I know there are at least *some* lessons, even in the present incomplete state of our knowledge. The players who began the second act—that of food-production—separately, in different parts of the world, were not all of one "pure race" nor did they have "pure" cultural traditions. Some apparently quite mixed Mediterraneans got off to the first start on the second act and brought it to its first two climaxes as well. Peoples of quite different physical type achieved the first climaxes in China and in the New World.

In our British example of how the late prehistory of Europe worked, we listed a continuous series of "invasions" and "reverberations." After each of these came fusion. Even though the Channel protected Britain from some of the extreme complications of the mixture and fusion of continental Europe, you can see how silly it would be to refer to a "pure" British race or a "pure" British culture. We speak of the United States as a "melting pot." But this is nothing new. Actually, Britain and all the rest of the world have been "melting pots" at one time or another.

By the time the written records of Mesopotamia and Egypt begin to turn up in number, the climaxes there are well under way. To understand the beginnings of the climaxes, and the real beginnings of the second act itself, we are thrown back on prehistoric archeology. And this is as true for China, India, Middle America, and the Andes, as it is for the Near East.

There are lessons to be learned from all of man's past, not simply lessons of how to fight battles or win peace conferences, but of how human society evolves from one stage to another. Many of these lessons can only be looked for in the prehistoric past. So far, we have only made a beginning. There is much still to do, and many gaps in the story are yet to be filled. The prehistorian's job is to find the evidence, to fill the gaps, and to discover the lessons men have learned in the past. As I see it, this is not only an exciting but a very practical goal for which to strive.

List of Books

BOOKS OF GENERAL INTEREST

(Chosen from a variety of the increasingly useful list of cheap paper-bound books.)

Childe, V. Gordon
What Happened in History. 1954. Penguin.
Man Makes Himself. 1955. Mentor.
The Prehistory of European Society. 1958. Penguin.

Dunn, L. C., and Dobzhansky, Th.
Heredity, Race, and Society. 1952. Mentor.

Frankfort, Henri, Frankfort, H. A., Jacobsen, Thorkild, and Wilson, John A.
Before Philosophy. 1954. Penguin.

Simpson, George G.
The Meaning of Evolution. 1955. Mentor.

Wheeler, Sir Mortimer
Archaeology from the Earth. 1956. Penguin.

GEOCHRONOLOGY AND THE ICE AGE

(Two general books. Some Pleistocene geologists disagree with Zeuner's interpretation of the dating evidence, but their points of view appear in professional journals, in articles too cumbersome to list here.)

Flint, R. F.
Glacial Geology and the Pleistocene Epoch. 1947. John Wiley and Sons.

Zeuner, F. E.
Dating the Past. 1952 (3rd ed.). Methuen and Co.

FOSSIL MEN AND RACE

(The points of view of physical anthropologists and human paleon-tologists are changing quickly. Different points of view are listed here.)

Boule, Marcellin, and Vallois, Henri V.
Fossil Men. 1957. Dryden Press.

Clark, W. E. Le Gros
History of the Primates. 1956 (5th ed.). British Museum (Natural History). (Also in Phoenix edition, 1957.)

Coon, Carleton S.
The Origin of Races. 1962. Alfred A. Knopf, Inc. (A useful index of human fossils but with highly controversial interpretations.)

Dobzhansky, Theodosius
Mankind Evolving. 1962. Yale University Press. (Called "a great book" by some anthropologists.)

GENERAL ANTHROPOLOGY

(These are standard texts not absolutely up to date in every detail, or interpretative essays concerned with cultural change through time as well as in space.)

Kroeber, A. L.
Anthropology. 1948. Harcourt, Brace.

Linton, Ralph
The Tree of Culture. 1955. Alfred A. Knopf, Inc.

Redfield, Robert
The Primitive World and Its Transformations. 1953. Cornell University Press. (Also in Cornell paperbacks edition.)

Steward, Julian H.
Theory of Culture Change. 1955. University of Illinois Press.

White, Leslie
The Science of Culture. 1949. Farrar, Strauss. (Also in Evergreen edition.)

GENERAL PREHISTORY

(A sampling of the more useful and current standard works in English.)

Braidwood, R. J., and Willey, G. R.
Courses toward Urban Life. 1962. Viking Fund Publications in Anthropology, no. 32; also Aldine Press. (A collection of essays by specialists.)

Childe, V. Gordon

The Dawn of European Civilization. 1957. Kegan Paul, Trench, Trubner.

Prehistoric Migrations in Europe. 1950. Instituttet for Sammenlignende Kulturforskning.

Clark, Grahame

Archaeology and Society. 1957. Harvard University Press. (Also in University paperbacks edition.)

World Prehistory: an Outline. 1961. Cambridge University Press. (A useful paperback but highly compressed with facts; somewhat soporific.)

Clark, J. G. D.

Prehistoric Europe: The Economic Basis. 1952. Methuen and Co.

Garrod, D. A. E.

Environment, Tools, and Man. 1946. Cambridge University Press.

Movius, Hallam L., Jr.

"Old World Prehistory: Paleolithic" in *Anthropology Today.* Kroeber, A. L., ed. 1953. University of Chicago Press.

Oakley, Kenneth P.

Man the Tool-Maker. 1956. British Museum (Natural History). (Also in Phoenix edition, 1957.)

Piggott, Stuart

British Prehistory. 1949. Oxford University Press.

Piggott, Stuart (editor.)

The Dawn of Civilization. 1961. Thames and Hudson, Ltd. (The best of the large and costly picture books, with brief, somewhat journalistic texts.)

Pittioni, Richard

· *Die Urgeschichtlichen Grundlagen der Europäischen Kultur.* 1949. Deuticke. (A single book which attempts to cover the whole range of European prehistory to ca. 1 A.D.)

THE NEAR EAST

Adams, Robert M.

"Developmental Stages in Ancient Mesopotamia," *in* Steward, Julian, *et al, Irrigation Civilizations: A Comparative Study.* 1955. Pan American Union.

Braidwood, Robert J., Howe, Bruce, *et al.*

Prehistoric Investigations in Iraqi Kurdistan. 1960. University of Chicago Press.

Childe, V. Gordon
 New Light on the Most Ancient East. 1952. Oriental Dept., Routledge and Kegan Paul.

Frankfort, Henri
 The Birth of Civilization in the Near East. 1951. Indiana University Press. (Also in Anchor edition, 1956.)

Kraeling, Carl H., and Adams, Robert M. (editors)
 City Invincible. 1960. University of Chicago Press.

Pallis, Svend A.
 The Antiquity of Iraq. 1956. Munksgaard.

Wilson, John A.
 The Burden of Egypt. 1951. University of Chicago Press. (Also in Phoenix edition, called *The Culture of Ancient Egypt,* 1956.)

HOW DIGGING IS DONE

Braidwood, Linda
 Digging beyond the Tigris. 1953. Schuman, New York.

Braidwood, Robert J.
 Archeologists and What They Do. 1960. Franklin Watts, Inc.

Wheeler, Sir Mortimer
 Archaeology from the Earth. 1954. Oxford University Press, London.

Index

Abbevillian, 48; core-biface tool, 44, 48
Acheulean, 48, 60, 61
Acheuleo-Levalloisian, 63
Acheuleo-Mousterian, 63
Adams, R. M., 106
Adzes, 45
Africa, east, 67, 89; north, 70, 89; south, 22, 25, 34, 40, 67
Agriculture, incipient, in England, 141; in Near East, 123
Ain Hanech, 48
Amber, taken from Baltic to Greece, 168
American Indians, 90, 143
Anatolia, used as route to Europe, 138
Animals, in caves, 55, 64; in cave art, 85
Antevs, Ernst, 19
Anyathian, 47
Archeological interpretation, 8
Archeology, defined, 8
Architecture, at Jarmo, 128; at Jericho, 133
Arrow, points, 94; shaft straightener, 83
Art, in caves, 84; East Spanish, 85; figurines, 84; Franco-Cantabrian, 84, 85; movable (engravings, modeling, scratchings), 83, 84; painting, 83; sculpture, 83
Asia, western, 67
Assemblage, defined, 14; European, 94; Jarmo, 129; Maglemosian, 94; Natufian, 113
Aterian, industry, 67; point, 89
Australopithecinae, 24
Australopithecine, 22, 25, 26
Awls, 77
Axes, 62, 94
Ax-heads, 15
Azilian, 97
Aztecs, 146

Baghouz, 153
Bakun, 135
Baltic sea, 93

Banana, 107
Barley, wild, 109
Barrow, 142
Battle-axe folk, 165; assemblage, 165
Beads, 80; bone, 114
Beaker folk, 165; assemblage, 165–166
Bear, in cave art, 85; cult, 68
Belgium, 94
Belt cave, 126
Bering Strait, used as route to New World, 98
Bison, in cave art, 85
Blade, awl, 77; backed, 75; blade-core, 71; end scraper, 77; stone, defined, 71; strangulated (notched), 76; tanged point, 76; tools, 71, 75–80, 90, 91; tool tradition, 70
Boar, wild, in cave art, 85
Bogs, source of archeological materials, 94
Bolas, 54
Bordes, François, 62
Borer, 77
Boskop skull, 34, 35
Bostanci, Enver, 113
Boyd, William C., 36
Bracelets, 118
Brain, development of, 24
Breadfruit, 107
Breasted, James H., 107
Brick, at Jericho, 133
Britain, 94; late prehistory, 164–176; invaders, 167
Broch, 173
Buffalo, in China, 55; killed by stampede, 86
Burials, 66, 86; in "henges," 165; in urns, 169
Burins, 75
Burma, 90
Byblos, 134

Camel, 55
Cannibalism, 55

Cattle, wild, 85, 112; in cave art, 85; domesticated, 16; at Skara Brae, 143
Caucasoids, 34
Cave men, 29
Caves, 62; art in, 84
Celts, 171–173
Chariot, 161
"Chellean" man, 26, 27
Chicken, domestication of, 107
Chiefs, in food-gathering groups, 68
Childe, V. Gordon, 8
China, 137
Choukoutien, 35
Choukoutienian, 47
Civilization, beginnings, 145–50, 158; meaning of, 145
Clactonian, 45, 47 52, 53
Clay, used in modeling, 128; baked, used for tools, 154
Club-heads, 94
Colonization, in America, 143; in Europe, 143
Combe Capelle, 30
Combe Capelle-Brünn group, 34
Commont, Victor, 51
Copper, 135
Corn, in America, 146
Corrals for cattle, 141
"Cradle of mankind," 137
Cremation, 169
Crete, 163
Cro-Magnon, 30, 34
Cultivation, incipient, 105, 109, 111
Culture, change, 99; characteristics, defined, 38, 49; prehistoric, 39

Danube Valley, used as route from Asia, 140
Dates, 157
Deer, 55, 96
Dog, domesticated, 96
Domestication, of animals, 100, 105, 107; of plants, 100
Drill, 77
Dubois, Eugene, 27

Early Dynastic Period, Mesopotamia, 148
East Spanish art, 72, 85
Egypt, 70, 126
Ehringsdorf, 31
Elephant, 55
Emiran flake point, 74
England, 164–170; prehistoric, 19, 40; farmers in, 140
Eoanthropus dawsoni, 29
Eoliths, 41
Eridu, 154, 156
Euphrates River, floods in, 149

Europe, cave dwellings, 58; at end of Ice Age, 93; early farmers, 140; glaciers in, 40; huts in, 86; routes into, 138–140; spread of food production to, 137

Far East, 69, 90
Farmers, 103
Fauresmith industry, 67
Fayum, 135; radiocarbon date, 147
"Fertile Crescent," 107, 147
Figurines, "Venus," 84; at Jarmo, 128; at Ubaid, 154
Fire, used by Peking man, 54
First Dynasty, Egypt, 148
Fish-hooks, 80, 94
Fishing, 80; by food-producers, 122
Fish lines, 80
Fish spears, 94
Flint industry, 127
Fontéchevade, 32, 56, 58, 59
Food-collecting, 104, 121; end of, 104
Food-gatherers, 53, 178
Food-gathering, 99, 104; in Old World, 104; stages of, 104
Food-producers, 178
Food-producing economy, 122; in America, 146; in Asia, 105
Food-producing revolution, 99, 105; causes of, 101; preconditions for, 100
Food-production, beginnings of, 99; carried to Europe, 110
Food-vessel folk, 166
"Forest folk," 97, 98, 104, 110
Fox, Sir Cyril, 176
France, caves in, 56

Galley Hill (fossil type), 29
Garrod, D. A., 73
Gazelle, 116
Germany, 94
Ghassul, 157
Glaciers, 18, 30; destruction by, 40
Goat, wild, 108; domesticated, 128
Grain, first planted, 21
Graves, passage, 142; gallery, 142
Greece, civilization in, 163; as route to western Europe, 138; towns in, 163
Grimaldi skeletons, 34

Haçilar 134, 138
Hackberry seeds used as food, 55
Halaf, 152; assemblage, 152
Hallstatt, tradition, 170, 171
Hand, development of, 24, 25
Hand adzes, 46
Hand axes, 44
Harpoons, antler, 83, 94; bone, 82, 94
Hassuna, 130; assemblage, 131, 132

Old World, 67, 70, 90; continental phases in, 18
Olorgesailie, 40, 51
Ostrich, in China, 55
Ovens, 128

Paintings in caves, 84, 85,
Paleoanthropic man, 50
Palestine, burials, 56; cave sites, 52; types of man, 69
Parpallo, 89
Patjitanian, 45, 47
Pebble tools, 42, 43
Peking cave, 54; animals in, 55
Peking man, 27, 28, 29, 54, 55, 58
Pendants, 80; bone, 114
Perrot, Jean, 113
Pestle, 114
Peterborough, 142
Pictographic signs, 160, 161
Pig, wild, 108
Piggot, S. 171, 174
"Piltdown, man," 29
Pins, 80
Pithecanthropus, 26, 27, 30
Pleistocene, 18, 25
Plows developed, 123
Points, arrow, 76; laurel leaf, 78; shouldered, 78, 79; split-based bone, 80, 82; tanged, 76; willow leaf, 78
Potatoes, in America, 146
Pottery, 122, 130, 154; decorated, 142; painted, 131, 152, 153; Susa style, 157; in tombs, 142
Prehistory, defined, 7; range of, 17
Pre-neanderthaloids, 30, 31, 36
Pre-Solutrean point, 89
Pre-Stellenbosch, 48
Proto-Literate assemblage, 158–162

Race, 35; biological, 36; "pure," 16
Radioactivity, 9, 10, 11
Radioactive carbon dates, 92, 130 135, 136, 158
Ras Shamra, 14
Redfield, Robert, 38, 49
Reed, C. A., 128
Reindeer, 94
Rhinoceros, 93; in cave art, 85
Rhodesian man, 32
Riss glaciation, 58
Rock-shelters, 58; art in, 85

Saccopastore, 31
Sahara Desert, 34, 102
Samarra, 153; pottery, 131, 153
Sangoan industry, 67
Sarab, 126, 130

Sauer, Carl, 137
Sbaikian point, 89
Schliemann, H., 12, 13
Scotland, 166, 171
Scraper, flake, 79; end scraper on blade, 77, 78; keel-shaped, 79, 80, 81
Sculpture in caves, 83
Sebilian III, 126
Shaheinab, 136
Sheep, wild, 108; at Skara Brae, 143; in China, 55
Shellfish, 143
Shimshara, 127
Ship, Ubaidian, 156
Sialk, 126, 135; assemblage, 135
Siberia, 88; pathway to New World, 98
Sickle, 112, 154; blade, 114, 130
Silo, 122
Sinanthropus, 27, 28, 35
Skara Brae, 143
Snails used as food, 128
Soan, 47
Solecki, R., 73, 116
Solo (fossil type), 29, 32
Solutrean industry, 77
Spear, shaft, 78; thrower, 82, 83
Speech, development of organs of, 25
Squash, in America, 146
Steinheim fossil skull, 28, 29
Stillbay industry, 67
Stonehenge, 167
Stratification, in caves, 15, 57; in sites, 12
Swanscombe (fossil type), 11, 28
Syria, 107
Syro-Cicilia, 134, 135, 138, 140

Tabun, 60, 71
Tardenoisian, 97
Taro, 107
Tasa, 136
Tayacian, 47, 59
Teeth, pierced, in beads and pendants, 114
Tell es-Sultan, 133
Temples, 123, 156
Tepe Asiab, 116, 119, 127
Tepe Gawra, 158
Ternafine, 28, 29
Teshik Tash, 69
Textiles, 122
Thong-stropper, 80
Tigris River, floods in, 149
Toggle, 80
Tomatoes, in America, 146
Tombs, megalithic, 142
Tool-making, 42, 49
Tool-preparation traditions, 65
Tools, 62; antler, 80; blade, 70, 71, 75: